SCOOTER NOMADS
BOOK TWO

SCOOTER NOMADS
BOOK TWO
OR
'WE DECIDED TO GIVE IT A GO'
... AGAIN!

BARDDRIEV PRESS

Copyright © Edsel F. Ward 2017

All rights reserved

First Edition
Paperback

ISBN: 978-0-9944992-8-8

Apart from any fair dealing for the purposes of private study, research or review, as permitted under the Copyright Act, no part of this book may be reproduced by any process without permission. Copyright of all text and photographs resides under the Copyright, Designs and Patents Act with Edsel F. Ward.

Layout and Book Design: Brad Drew
Photographs and Maps: Edsel F. Ward
Cover Art and Design: Brad Drew

For my grandchildren,

in the hope that they will enjoy the adventures

of a past era and find their own sense of adventure

waiting within their own lives.

AUTHOR'S NOTE:

Photographs are later, black and white copies taken from the original 1960, 35mm colour transparencies made during the course of the scooter adventures. As might be expected, time has not been kind to the state of the original slides; but, nor do those locations appear the same now, as they did then.

TABLE OF CONTENTS :

Authors Note 6

Table of Contents 7

Acknowledgments 8

Forward 9

Introduction 13

Chapter One: Yugoslavia 15
    A Preambled Backtrack...............................

Chapter Two: Greece 23
    Turkey to Greece & Yugoslavia.....................

Chapter Three: Austria 53
    Austria, Switzerland, West & East Germany
    Denmark, Norway, Sweden & Denmark.......

Chapter Four: Holland 97
    Holland & Belgium ....

Chapter Five: France 109

Epilogue ... Post-Mirra: The UK 123

Addendum: A Photographic Summary ... 151

ACKNOWLEDGMENTS:

This book covers the second half of the journey made by Keith Bassett and myself in 1960, from (what was then called) Ceylon to France, where the scooter, 'Mirrabooka', broke down for the final time. The intention had been to get to London but it wasn't to be so ... the details follow in the course of the book.

On the 16th October 2012, Keith passed away at age 88, having spent most of his life travelling. Keith would work for a few years, save up and be off again. He saw most of the places he wanted to see but on a trip to the high Andes, was stopped because of ill health. As stated in Book 1, we were a good team and 'decided to give it a go'.

To my typist, Ailsa, who typed-up my scratchy, hand-written lead-pencil manuscript, with such speed and accuracy ... a very-grateful 'well-done' and thank you.

To Brad, editor and publisher, my sincere thanks, for the time spent putting everything: script, maps, photos and covers together, to make a book ... thank you, Brad.

To Lorraine and my family, who continually contributed time, advice and encouragement ... a big 'thank you'.

EDSEL WARD

Montville, Queensland

February, 2018

FOREWARD (Not Foreword):

As a small boy growing up in Morningside, Brisbane, in the 1970's, I would occasionally put on Edsel's (my Dad's) 'skid-lid' as he called it. It was the helmet he wore for this great adventure he and his bushwalking mate, Keith Bassett, undertook in the 1960's. Their plan was to ride their 200cc Japanese 'Rabbit' motor-scooter (christened 'Mirrabooka') from Ceylon to Turkey, then on through Europe ... which they did.

This would be a journey that covered 24,000 miles (38,625 kilometres), spanned twelve months and crossed two continents. Dad's skid-lid would sit in various spots around his 'home office' (as is the modern term), while he worked first as a timber representative for a Saw Mill and then later, running his own business. The helmet had no permanent home or place of honour to announce to everyone what it was, where it had travelled or the adventures it had seen.

It felt heavy, hard (in fact, granite-hard ... drop that helmet on your foot and you'd be off to hospital) and smelt of old, worn leather. Putting it on, nestling one's head into the webbing, adjusting the chin-strap, it was surprisingly-comfortable and reassuring. It had presence, telling you quietly that this skid-lid had seen and done A LOT!

This book continues where the first book, 'Scooter Nomads', finished, with Edsel and Keith arriving at the Bosphorus. This second volume of 'Scooter Nomads' covers the journey from Turkey into Europe. The journey now took the three adventurers ('Mirra', the scooter, now recognised as an essential and equal partner amongst the travellers) through Turkey, Greece, Yugoslavia, Austria, Switzerland, West Germany, Austria, East Germany, back into West Germany, Denmark, Norway, Sweden, back through Denmark and West Germany, then into Holland, Belgium and finally, to France. Without wishing to spoil the story, it was in France, that the trio was finally split, with 'Mirra' needing major repairs.

Both Keith and Edsel then moved on to the United Kingdom, where Edsel continued to roam whilst Keith, in urgent need of funds, went to work in a factory. All three were later reunited for the journey home to Australia.

'Scooter Nomads' was written from two diaries, written at the end of each day, fifty years ago. The adventure occurred during a time of immense change during the Cold War. It is interesting to read and reflect on the world as it was and compare to how it is currently ... and though time has passed and the places, peoples, cultures, ideologies and technologies have all changed, there is a beautiful narrative throughout the books, of the warmth people have for embracing the traveller and a reminder that people from all walks of life have more in common than in differences.

As an adult, it was my wish and an honour for me to finally meet Keith and later, to attend his funeral with Dad (Keith passed away on the 16th October 2012, aged 88 years). I grew up with the stories of that trip, which would come out when a memory was triggered, usually when Dad and I would be doing something together.

Significantly, both my parents instilled and shaped values that I myself and my siblings, share in common with that journey: a sense of humour, adaptability, resilience, a love of wild places and travel, an appreciation of natural history and of cultures ... and also, a desire to "Give It A Go".

GARETH WARD

Brisbane

7th April 2018

Edsel, Keith and Mirrabooka in Berlin

INTRODUCTION:

World War II had finished and the cold war had begun, with Germany being divided into East Germany controlled by the Russians and West Germany, controlled by America, Britain and France. Berlin was now in East Germany and divided into four sections: American, British, French and Russian.

Russia had a tight grip on Bulgaria, Albania and Yugoslavia (the name given to Marshal Tito's Balkan States); and Tito was controlled by Russia. Greece shared a long border with Bulgaria, Yugoslavia and Albania, their border being one large army camp.

Book One of this adventure, took us as far as Istanbul and the end of Asia. Crossing the Bosporus brought us into Europe and a gradual change as we moved north. We intended to see as much of Europe as possible on our 'Rabbit' 200cc fluid-drive, rear-wheeled, air-spring motor scooter. With a few alterations, it had served us well. Our proposed travels would take us through alpine country - Austria, Germany, north into Scandinavia (trying for North Cape in Norway), then south via Sweden, into the low countries, France and maybe Spain ...

That was the plan.

Leaving Turkey :

Ferries on The Bosphorus, Istanbul

CHAPTER ONE: YUGOSLAVIA

We were in mountainous southern Yugoslavia on a rough, gravel-corrugated, pot-holed road, when I heard a noise which sounded like a semi-trailer coming up fast behind us. I looked to my right and was startled to see a thumping great tank with a red star on the turret, crashing through the timber, about twenty yards away and parallel to the road.

Keith screamed out over the noise, "Crikey, they are on to us – and I haven't got my anti-tank gun."

Keith had been in an anti-tank platoon in Korea. He had shot at these tanks before and now, wanted his gun.

I screamed back at him, "Remember, we are on a scooter and we don't have room for an anti-tank gun. You will just have to wait until we get home."

The tank got ahead of us, then slewed across the road in front, blocking our path. I braked heavily and stopped just short of the monster.

The turret lid opened and an officer climbed out, followed by a crew member with a sub-machine gun. The officer greeted us with a grave, unblinking stare, then went through the language list and decided we spoke English.

Holding his hand out, he said, "Passport? Visa?"

We got our papers and handed them to him. He thumbed through them, snorted, handed them back and then in broken English said, "You have ridden into a Russian tank firing-range. We are about to start night exercises. You can go no further. You will camp the night right here. You will not move until daylight."

Climbing back into the tank, he repeated the warning. The crew member with the sub-machine gun followed him. The lid slammed shut and the dinosaur rattled off into the twilight.

We pitched our tent and cooked dinner, which consisted of tinned meat and rice, followed by dried fruit. We retired to our sleeping bags and waited for the exercises to start.

* * *

We now had time to recall the events since leaving Istanbul three weeks ago. In Istanbul, we had discovered that it had been given three names – Byzantium, Constantinople and then, Istanbul. These three names gave us a quick understanding of the long history of invasions and occupations of the city; and of the mixed cultures. There had been plenty to see and do but because of a Greek visa with a date on it, we couldn't spend too much time in one place ... we had to keep moving.

I'd found the city huge and overpowering – everything was so big. We did however, go back to one of the famous seven hills of Istanbul, which overlooked the city and the Bosporus and there, took a photo on that fine, clear morning. Then, it was off to the ferry, driving over cobble-stone streets and later, a choppy ride on the ferry in clear, cold air.

We had travelled around the Sea of Marmara to Tekirdag and were looking forward to visiting the Gallipoli Peninsula; but when we got to the turn-off, we found the road was closed with road signs and a lollypop man, who waved us away. The road was being rebuilt and we would not have got far with our small wheels. We decided to move on and continued straight ahead, towards the border.

We had been told that the following day was Turkey's national day and to be prepared for holdups and other unexpected things.

It was a slow trip around the Sea of Marmara, brought about by dirty petrol. We'd had the scooter serviced in Istanbul and everything appeared fine but once on the road, the dirty fuel caught up with us. It was stop, clean up ... then off again, then stop. It gradually cleaned-up but it took a while. Fuel out of 44 gallon drums had been a problem on and off, for the whole trip. We were looking forward to Europe, where we could fuel up at a proper fuel pump, at a proper service station.

We had camped the night in a beautiful spot by a clear, running stream in a sheltered, well-treed area. It had a fireplace, with stacks of firewood nearby. We put the tent up, cooked dinner on the fireplace, then crawled into the sleeping bags. That night was one of the coldest we had had since leaving the desert country – it was freezing. In any-case, it had been one way of preparing us for things to come.

Next morning, we had set off for the border, which was about 16kms away. The air was clean and crisp and I was wondering what time the parades would start, as I didn't have a Turkish early-morning clock. When we crested a long, uphill rise, we were stopped by an army checkpoint with some high-ranking officers in charge.

Another group of officers were standing around a table under a large tent with no sides. The table had a big map on it and they were studying it closely, talking and waving their arms and looking at their watches. Then one of the officers stepped forward and indicated to us to proceed down the road.

It was only then, that I saw what was on the road ahead: it was lined with small tanks, troops, people in national dress ... and lots of bunting. I started the motor and moved out. Immediately, people started cheering and waving flags at us. As we rode, the troops stood to attention; some saluted, with Keith returning the salute.

Then the penny dropped - all of the looking at the watches bit, meant someone was running late and we were being sent through as a distraction, until the main cavalcade arrived. Someone in that tent had a sense of humour! I thought, "Right, this is something we had never done"; so I decided to give them a good show and rode slowly, giving people plenty of time to wave their flags and cheer ... and we even received some flowers in return.

Then I wondered about the real cavalcade: if there would be any cheering and bunting left for them? I hoped there was some left for them, as we now seemed to be using it all up. We had been told to expect the unexpected ... and it had happened.

Then I heard Keith, sitting behind me say, "We should contact the mayor and thank him, for the send off."

Suddenly it was all over, as we burst into the countryside of wavering wheat. We stopped at Edirne for lunch, before proceeding to the border and Customs, where there were laid-back border guards: two leaning on a post, the others leaning on their rifles. We were put straight through.

Keith, the Jouster of Tanks, in Yugoslavia

From Istanbul to Yugoslavia

King Phillip of Greece, Lion Statue: Near Alexandroupoli

Keith on the waterfront at Alexandroupoli

CHAPTER TWO

GREECE

We were now in Greece and, riding along, we heard church bells for the first time in a long while and only then, we realised it was Sunday.

We were made welcome by people showering flower petals over us – not at all like it had been with the small boys in Persia and Turkey, where they would shower us with rocks. The help of Australian troops during the war-time invasion of Greece, was still fresh in the minds of people and, being recognised as Aussies, we were made welcome.

We had breakfast at a roadside café, where we met an English boy who believed he could get to Australia on five pounds. We wished him luck.

We had entered country which was full of ancient history, archaeology, ruins and rugged terrain. The first major town was Alexandroupoli on the Aegean Sea. The town is not far from the Turkish border and faces the Gallipoli Peninsula. The long waterfront esplanade with closely-packed shops, made a lovely picture, with a mountainous backdrop directly behind the town.

Amongst the shops, we found a cake shop and had morning tea. As the towns name suggests, it was named after Alexander the Great, in the third century BC.

We had our second flat tyre for the morning, right in front of the King Phillip of Greece lion statue, making us stop and pay homage to the King – that is, reading the memorial script while mending the tyre.

Riding on to a very scenic lookout, we had parked to admire the view, when a dark-grey panel van pulled in near us. We had seen this van on and off for the past four days and had made comment about his following us.

The driver alighted from the van, nodded to us and sauntered over. He was well-dressed, in a grey suit the same colour as the panel van, giving the impression he was a businessman.

No introductions were made and he asked, "Where have you come from and where are you going?" We told him.

Then he asked, "Would you like to earn some money?"

We asked, "What would one do to earn money?"

The answer was, "Gun-running in Yugoslavia." He opened up one of the doors of the van to reveal a load of weapons.

We said, "No. Why don't you take them?"

He replied, "I have a lot of orders to deliver and need help. There is good money to be made and you wouldn't need your scooter."

We said, "Look, we are on holidays and we don't work on holidays."

He then started quoting big dollars to do the job, making us more suspicious. Keith and I looked at each other, shook our heads, then climbed on Mirrabooka and rode off.

I said to Keith, "I bet those guns are not for Yugoslavia. He wouldn't have told us unless we said yes." Having an adventure is one thing but getting locked up or shot, is another.

This was the third occasion we had been approached about gun- running: once had been in India and once, in Pakistan ... and the people concerned had looked a bit like him. Our general appearance probably made us a target ... but it was interesting to know what goes on.

* * *

The next big city in the north was Thessaloniki: a bigger version of our morning-tea stop and named after King Phillip's fourth son; and a brother to Alexander. We had to be aware of the hidden army camps on the long border with Turkey, Bulgaria, Yugoslavia and Albania. There was activity, twenty-four/seven and it was impossible to sleep past pre-dawn, as the troops went for their morning run; then the ground would tremble and the trees would shake.

Travelling towards Athens, we passed in the shadow of Mt Olympus – according to the map, 2917 metres high and home to the Greek Gods. Looking at the peak, we were tempted to go climbing but when we found out that we would first have to go to Athens, to get a permit and a guide, we lost interest. Besides, Greece is not short on mountains and rugged terrain as it is at the southern end of the Balkan Peninsula and only a quarter of the land is suitable for agriculture.

It was another hot day and, riding towards Athens, we could see the heat haze hovering over the city. On entering the city, it looked tired and needful of a lot of work. The road was reasonable and the traffic heavy. After spending a lot of time in open country, I now had to switch on all my city senses to cope with loaded, heavy trucks, screaming cars and motor bikes. There seemed to be no road rules and of course, we were moving slower than the rest of them: which told me, we should park the scooter and walk, or use local transport.

We had a youth hostel membership and noted there was one in Athens. After a little help, we found the hostel. It was a nice building: four floors, I recall, and it had good amenities. Looking at the guests and the number of countries they came from, it had to be presentable.

We booked in and discovered that there were lots of Americans, Germans, English and four Aussies ... the first we had seen since Colombo; and we had now clocked up 22,530 kilometres and were still ticking over after a few major problems earlier on (Refer Book 1). Management gave us a cubicle to park Mirrabooka; then we set off on foot to explore.

It was good that we were acclimatised to the heat and the dust so they didn't bother us. We found it wasn't until late afternoon and evening, that people emerged from hiding ... then, the streets and lane-ways became crowded and unless we knew where we were going, we would have been trampled underfoot.

The first things we had wished to see were the Acropolis and the Parthenon but we found that both buildings were under reconstruction, with scaffolding for the workers. They had been neglected for years and the war had not helped. We had seen pictures of them before but seeing them in real life put everything into perspective.

The place was crawling with tourists. We visited several museums and the time spent in them gave us a break from the traffic. We visited museums and art galleries, in order to get a feel for Greek history and a culture, 4000 years old.

I found myself looking at one display regarding the theatre of Epidaurus, built in the fourth century BC, with perfect acoustics and architectural harmony ... and with a seating capacity for 14,000 spectators – ideal for ancient drama; and that was only one of the many such theatres ... making them superior in many ways, to the acoustics of modern-day theatre venues.

Visiting some of these sites, this all became very real – that is, how well, the acoustics worked. I do a bit of wood carving and at the time, I could admire their stone carving with the tools of their day and appreciate, how well they understood the stone.

A visit to the palace proved entertaining, watching the Changing of the Guard with Evzones (the Palace Guards) doing their routine, in their very-unique uniform: hats, white frilled skirts and stockings, shoes with red pompoms on their toes and their stylised, slow movement ... they had us absolutely fascinated.

On one occasion at the Parthenon, an air-conditioned bus pulled up and unloaded its passengers: all very-wealthy, over-middle-aged Americans. On exiting the bus, the heat hit them and half of them climbed back into the bus. One of them managed to stagger over to us, leaning heavily on his walking stick with sweat pouring off him.

"Where are you from, Sonny?" I told him Australia and why we were here.

To which he replied, "I wish I were you. Look at me ... a multi-millionaire and I can hardly walk or breathe. Don't get rich Sonny – it will ruin your health. Enjoy it, now."

* * *

There are around 2000 islands around Greece but only 160 are inhabited and, having heard so much about them, we had to at least pay some, a visit. The larger ones like Rhodes, Corfu and others, were out for us because we were tight on money; so we decided to look at closer islands: Andros, Kea and Aegina, which had a one and a half hour ferry trip from Piraeus. While boarding the ferry, we met Don again, whom we had last seen in Istanbul and invited him to join us.

The weather was very hot and dry; and the locals and tourists had all taken refuge indoors. We broke the mould and did a 16 km hike across the island to a lovely bay with quaint houses dotted around and met up with two Aussies, Ian and Col, making-up a party of five. We had a fish dinner, followed by Greek pastry. The beautiful, clear-blue water kept us fresh for the hike back to catch the ferry. It was a highlight, to streak out in such lovely surroundings.

On the way back to Piraeus, we passed a dry dock which was lit up by welding flashes. Several big oceangoing liners had just arrived and spilt their cargo into the port. There were people everywhere, so we all decided to take refuge in a cinema. Like most cinemas Keith and I had visited, it was all drama but ours had been 'Bourke and Hare, Grave Diggers'.

The last time we had been to the movies was in India and Pakistan, where friendly, movie-crazy locals insisted that we must see these particular movies and we felt obliged to go with them, as they had been most helpful to us in many ways. These visits had been an experience ... the cinemas were massive shelter sheds and the venues were packed with seating on long lines of timber forms to cater for the masses ... and the air-conditioning was on only when there was a breeze. This was in early Bollywood days.

Greek cinemas were in proper buildings, with ceiling fans and in our case, a good sea breeze. We had dinner and agreed to meet the boys next day to look at the markets.

Next morning, we took the tube to the markets and for us, they were a real eye opener. The first building we saw, was a meat market and it was huge. I had never seen a building so full of meat in all stages, from carcass through to ready-to-cook and eat ... as well as all the noise and activity that went with it. We moved on, into fruit and vegetables – a vast building, with all manner of produce. A lot of this would have come in from the islands and the markets, being close to the wharf, kept everything fresh.

Seafood was next and I saw fish of all shapes and sizes, octopus of every size, squid and shellfish. Next, was leather work; then clothes, shoes and so on. There were buyers aplenty. When we had had enough, we found a seafood place by the water: a lovely setting, with views out over the sea.

It had been an interesting time in the market. It had also been good catching up with Don, Ian and Col. As we were all heading in the same general direction, we looked forward to our next meeting, with more stories to exchange.

* * *

The road to Corinth was very spectacular and windy on the rugged, rocky winding road, making a wonderful foreground to the ancient ruins of Delphi on the slopes, where they looked stunning. Along the way, roads were lined with gum trees, making us feel very much at home. Other trees included oleanders, lemon, cherries, loquats, apricots and grapes.

The ferry crossing, on the western side of the gulf, was very rough due to the clash of currents, east-west and west-east; and when they met, there was much turbulence. We were pleased to get to the other shore.

Back on land, we then travelled north, across fertile, undulating farming country, with mile upon mile of orchards with plums, apricots, apples and cherries; all with laden branches, some overhanging the road and in their shade, we made a refreshing stop.

Further north, it was wilder country, with deep gorges and raging rivers, waterfalls and snow-capped, limestone mountains, rising to 2627 metres.

We turned east into drier country, to discover Meteora: a place of sheer columns of dark-grey rock, scattered over the landscape; all of this, created by wave action, millions of years ago. Perched on top of twenty-four of these masses of rock, were high, lofty monasteries built by monks who weren't afraid of heights and with the aid of ropes, ladders, stairs and tunnels and anything else that was available, built them in the fourteenth century.

At the time of our visit, the number had dropped from twenty-four to twelve. With the aid of a monk, we were able to explore two of them, which made an exciting and very scenic tour. We were taken up to the buildings in the traditional way, in a basket lifted by a windlass. That gave us good viewing of the cliffs and countryside. The caves, which had been shaped into the grey rock, were quite large and created a good living space made comfortable. Frescos and icons decorated the walls.

The land below had been cleared and olive trees planted, which prevented the soil from making the surrounding land, a desert.

We now turned north towards the Dinaric Alps, where we camped north of Arta, on flat country surrounded by wheat and poppies. Next morning we awoke early, to find lots of girls busy, harvesting the red poppies and we wondered where was their destination?

We rode to Florina: the last Greek town before Yugoslavia; then Bitola, where we changed money and finished up with a great wad of paper, not worth very much. We had been warned not to take too much out of the country, as it would not buy anything, anywhere else.

* * *

On entering Yugoslavia, we had moved back in time – to when the Ottoman Turks had occupied the Balkans and churches were replaced by mosques; and the men wore long, baggy pants, turned-up pointy shoes and turbans; and the women were completely covered. The main transport was horse and cart, some of the carts being huge, with outward-sloping sides and taking up a lot of room on the narrow, shell- and bomb-cratered roads. We bought fuel at Skopje, a town that had a different feel about it. The people looked war-weary but friendly. There seemed to be nothing happening; people were just wandering around in a daze. The forest-covered mountains were a picture, with wildflowers scattered over the green; then it was north, to Pec, where we had good views of the snow-capped peaks, viewed through the green forests.

From Pec to Andrijevica, was the most spectacular part of the run. Following a river gorge, with high, vertical cliffs either side and the road meandering along, under huge overhangs all the time, the alpine scenery got better ... and snow was falling.

After a while however, I said to Keith, "What's that noise?"

He replied, "That's gunfire – I would know that anywhere."

That gunfire kept up, on and off all day, echoing around the mountains. It was hard to tell where it was coming from. Later in the day, when the sound changed to rat-tat-tat, Keith shouted in my ear, "That's a heavy machine-gun. Someone is playing with seriously-heavy armaments. I don't like that – and what's worse, I don't know which way they are pointing them. We have no where to go but on this road; but we do have plenty of cover."

Bridges there, had had no repairs since World War II and crossing them, took time. Later that afternoon, we came to the scenario which I mentioned in the introduction to this book: in a tent, with unseen tanks somewhere behind us, waiting to start night exercises. It was dark when the first salvos went over. We didn't know how many tanks there were but there were certainly more than one; although they were way behind us and off to our right – and that put us on the edge of their line of fire.

Keith had been giving a commentary on their firing and manoeuvres, followed by, "I hope they can shoot straight."

We could hear the salvos going over; then, when the firing stopped, we could hear them change position. This went on until 2 am, when all became quiet ... then, the heavy machine-guns opened up. All of this noise was what we had been hearing, for the past few days. Before dawn, came another quiet. Then we heard the tanks rattle off ... then, a final silence.

Keith hadn't slept much during the night, as he was busy reliving past battles. I'd had broken sleep. It was like sleeping beside a railway line, with a train coming through every ten minutes. I had never served in the forces but it gave me some idea of what it would have been like. Marshal Tito, with his Russian connection, had given the Russians a free-run of the country; to carry out their exercises ... and they were taking full advantage of it.

* * *

Daylight came and we were on the move again. I rode slowly, so as to drink in this rugged scenery; then we started climbing through steep passes into alpine country. Travel was slow, as I had to pay attention to the road and remember that I had rucksacks on either side, extending out past the width of the scooter. The road wound between cliff faces and I was pleased that we seemed to have the road to ourselves. I had no idea of which way the tanks had gone.

All this while, we were climbing steadily – then, light snow started to fall. As we reached the snow line, we could see fingers of snow, running in gullies on the mountainsides. Suddenly, we hit a whiteout as a breeze got up and visibility dropped. I had to pull over until it passed ... I could not see the road ahead at all.

Riding on, we passed several burnt-out dwellings, which were now changing their black, burnt-out frames to white. The snow became heavier.

Near the top of a rise, we came to a burnt-out church, with stout walls intact but with very-little roof left. As the snow was getting heavier and the air, a lot colder, we considered moving into the ruin. On the other side of the road, was another road, leading up to a knoll with a building on top. We decided to investigate.

Riding up the rough road, we discovered that the building was a tavern and well lit-up. We parked under cover and walked to the big, wooden front door. From inside, we could hear singing. The building was built of pine logs and as we opened the door, we were greeted by a blast of hot air from a big stone fireplace on the other side of the building. The roof was held up by large timber posts, supporting the beams and roof.

There were about twenty people sitting around timber tables but another ten men, dressed in Yugoslavian army uniforms, sat in one corner of the room around a table filled with empty bottles ... and they were singing in full harmony, making a beautiful sound. More bottles of vodka were put on the table and then the volume went up. We found a table and enjoyed the singing.

A thick beef stew and pea soup were being served, along with coffee in brass cups. We paid up and ordered our meal. This was a real treat and we made the most of it. I was curious to know where the people came from, as we had seen little or no life around but the tavern appeared to be a focal point, since the location was at the top of an alpine pass.

I learnt the next day, that there was a sizeable town down in the next valley: and with that, it then all made good sense.

The meal was so good, we lined up for seconds. We might be needing this to keep us warm. The singing continued but one by one, the choir slowly slid under the table, leaving three who decided they should find a proper bed ... and left.

It was time for us to make a move. We enquired about another two beds but we were told that they were full up; so we decided to go back to the church. We were able to drive the scooter into the building – under what roof was left and set up in a sheltered corner. There were some timber planks, which we laid on the concrete floor for insulation. With the scooter for a wind-break and a tarp over the top, we were quite snug.

* * *

The next morning, it was fine – breakfast was followed by the long, downhill run to the village in the valley, where there appeared to be a festival on. In the village centre, there were about forty horses milling around, with riders dressed in mediaeval costume: some in leathers, others in chain mail. All had helmets of various sorts. It looked like they were ready for battle, with sabres swinging off their belts and lances in their hands. Women and villagers were dancing in the town square and the buildings were decorated with bunting.

We rode past the cavalry but, just as we cleared them, they lined up in two columns and cantered off in our direction. The two lines split to go left and right of us, making us 'piggy in the middle'. Moving quickly, they waved their lances over our heads as they passed. I felt we were going to be part of a tent-pegging exhibition.

Keith said in my ear, "I hope those horses don't stumble ... their lances might take our heads off."

About half the column had passed, when I saw where they were heading. There was a large sports ground off to our left, with tents set up on the far side. The lead horse peeled off and the rest followed. I was wondering if any of last night's singers were in the troop. When we were in the clear, I wished them luck, for ahead, there was a big, black cloud, full of lightning ... a storm was coming.

We started looking for shelter and rode along the lee side of a now-familiar mountain road, which was joined by a fast-flowing stream. In the past, the stream had covered the road and scoured out the opposite cliff face, creating an overhang and shelter from the rain.

For us, it was the perfect place to stop until the storm passed. We were not the first to use the shelter, for a fireplace had been made and firewood stacked for travellers.

We had just got ourselves in, when the heavens opened up and it rained all night. We cooked dinner on the fireplace; then rolled into our sleeping bags, where we slept well. We wondered how the pageant had fared in the storm.

Come next morning, the cloud was down and we could barely see past the length of the scooter. Then the cloud lifted and we were on a steep, long downhill run over lots of pot-holes and broken bridges to Pec, in Kosovo ... and the scenery, in the rain-washed air, was brilliant. We weren't aware of it at the time but we were only a short distance from Europe's version of the Grand Canyon in the USA. It was the Tara Canyon: 82 kilometres long and 1300 metres deep – in such mountainous country as might house a canyon.

The town was full of army personnel, trucks, and medium-sized tanks (not like the big Russian ones). We rode from Pec to Andrijevica, where we had an enormous lunch for 3 shillings in a café – then it was back uphill to 2448 metres, along an alpine road which turned towards the coast and a fjord-like approach to Dubrovnik – after that, we had another, very-steep, long downhill run to sea level. The scenery on the way down made a brilliant foreground to the Adriatic Sea.

* * *

Dubrovnik was a mediaeval fortified city made to keep pirates out, with high stone walls and turrets ... the red of the roof tiles made a colourful contrast against the blue sky and water. With the narrow cobblestone streets and tall buildings, it made for an interesting walk and we spent some time exploring. There was very little building outside the walls, which were patrolled by army men with sub-machine guns. We were summarily accosted by two of them.

"Want to see your passports."

"Why?"

"You have parked illegally and you will have to pay a fine."

"You want to see our passports for that? Could we speak to your commanding officer?"

While he was making up his mind, we climbed onto Mirrabooka, who carried us away very quickly.

We had ridden about five kilometres, when there was a large clunk from the rear wheel. We glided to a halt in front of a house. I was inspecting the scooter when the owner of the house came out to see what the trouble was.

"We have a broken chain for a start ... and the axle doesn't look too good."

At this, the house owner said, "There is a workshop in the town, just over the hill and by the sea. It's getting late and I suggest you spend the night in my barn; then, you can get a truck to take the scooter into the workshop in the morning."

We agreed and were invited to share a fish dinner with them as they had caught a lot of fish that day. We set up in the barn for the night, then had our fish dinner, which was delicious and with plenty of it. There were mum, dad and three children. After that the vodka came out – we felt uncomfortable with the wife and kids there, so we made our excuses and departed for the barn. As we left, we gave the wife some money, which she thankfully received ... and immediately hid. I don't think she had ever received money like this.

Next morning, I left Keith with 'Mirra' and walked to the town, which I found wasn't far if I took a ferry ride across the inlet which divided the town. I found the workshop and arranged for their truck to pick up the scooter and bring it back to the workshop. I went with the truck, which had given us five men to lift the scooter onto the truck. Before leaving, the owner gave us a bottle of local wine, telling us how good it was - "It will make you strong." - it looked like kerosene to me.

With neither Keith nor I being drinkers, Keith said to me, "What are you going to do with it? We don't have much room."

I said to him, "I think it could work well in our metho burner," ... and it did, in fact - we cooked our porridge on it every morning, to Norway and back.

With 'Mirra' loaded, we set off to the workshop. On inspection, we found that the spline had been stripped, which meant a new axle.

The mechanic said, "We can make one but it will take two or three days."

As we couldn't go anywhere without an axle, I said, "Go ahead."

The little town had a caravan and camping-park just across the road from the workshop and the camp ground had a water frontage onto the inlet. Perfect! It was a beautiful setting ... the inlet had sailing boats bobbing about and the campground was like a park.

We were pitching our tent, when a Dutch couple, camping nearby, came and introduced themselves ... and as we had no transport, asked if we would like a tour of the area. We said, "Yes please."

On returning to the park, we met up with an old Danish sea captain who, with his wife, invited us to share a meal with them. Lars proved to be good company and told us stories of his sailing days aboard the last of the big windjammers (sailing ships). He had sailed around the globe several times and talked of hurricanes and storms shredding their rigging, while trying not to lose their cargo on the Australia-Pacific run. Lars invited us to call in, when we were in Denmark and catch up with news of our trip.

While waiting for the axle, we did a little sailing, swimming and fishing, catching enough fish to cook our own fish and chip dinner. Dubrovnik was our holiday camp ... however, my only t-shirt was taken from the tent by somebody who kindly left swimming trunks in its place - his top was needing to be covered more than his bottom, it seemed!

With a new axle and chain, we were on the road again; on the tourist strip to Split, another walled city with narrow, cobblestone streets but with a big harbour, with lots of ferries darting about. Split was a lot bigger than Dubrovnik and more commercial, with fishing fleets and tour boats. This fortified town, with its waterfront stone walls, told the story of pirate days. History tells us that this coast was a wild place and a place where money had changed hands, with fortunes to be made and lost. But it still had its beauty and history, making it a place which would be good to revisit and have plenty of time to explore.

* * *

There is an island off the coast, Maribor, which is thought to be magnetic, as ships have compass problems when passing.

We now had to decide which way to travel - via Austria or Italy? Keith had a niece, married to a West-German, who lived in Berlin and we had been invited to pay a visit and stay awhile, which meant we should exit into Austria. An invitation like this should not be missed as Keith was part of the family.

From Split to Trogir, we passed many beautiful lakes; then turned back into the gaunt, grey, jagged Dinaric Alps, where the wind was howling beneath an ashen, damp sky and a corkscrew gravel road wound its way upwards, giving us spectacular views. It was late afternoon, when we found another unused church with half a roof and windproof walls. We booked in for the night!

This was indeed, a bleak place and we thanked our chain and axel for breaking in Dubrovnik and not up here. There was no sign of life anywhere.

The dusty, corkscrew road dropped down to Una National Park: a place of yellow wild flowers and lavender. Then we discovered Prijepolja National Park: a huge limestone mantle, with terraced, emerald and deep-blue lakes, fed by dozens of waterfalls; all of this, surrounded by lush green fir-forest. Uphill from the lakes, there was a big limestone cave system which appeared to be extensive. Only a few of them had been developed for tourists, with steps and handrails and lighting.

We walked the tracks and found the lakes, waterfalls and caves spectacular in their own right. The area was a jewel, set amongst the green forest and snow-capped mountains. We also found a National Park notice advising that black bear, deer and trout were within the area. We rode to two ski resorts, which turned out to be lavish and it was hard to believe that we were in the same country as the south, where we had been travelling.

Then it was downhill to Zagreb, the capital of Slovenia and a surprise. We had been in the wilderness for too long and now gazed at a well-laid-out city, with wide streets, parks and gardens, trams and tall buildings. At the time of our visit, all was quiet, with not many people around and no shops open ... and signs of war damage still evident.

We walked along some of the streets and decided that we had come on the wrong day but we found the wide fast-flowing Sava River with its big bridges, looking most-impressive.

We were now moving out of Yugoslavia and in some ways, we were sorry to leave this rugged, mountainous country with all of its diverse peoples, all held together by Marshal Tito.

Mount Olympus, Greece

Meteora, in Greece

Mountaintop Monastries at Meteora, in Greece

State of the roads in Southern Yugoslavia

Local transport in Southern Yugoslavia

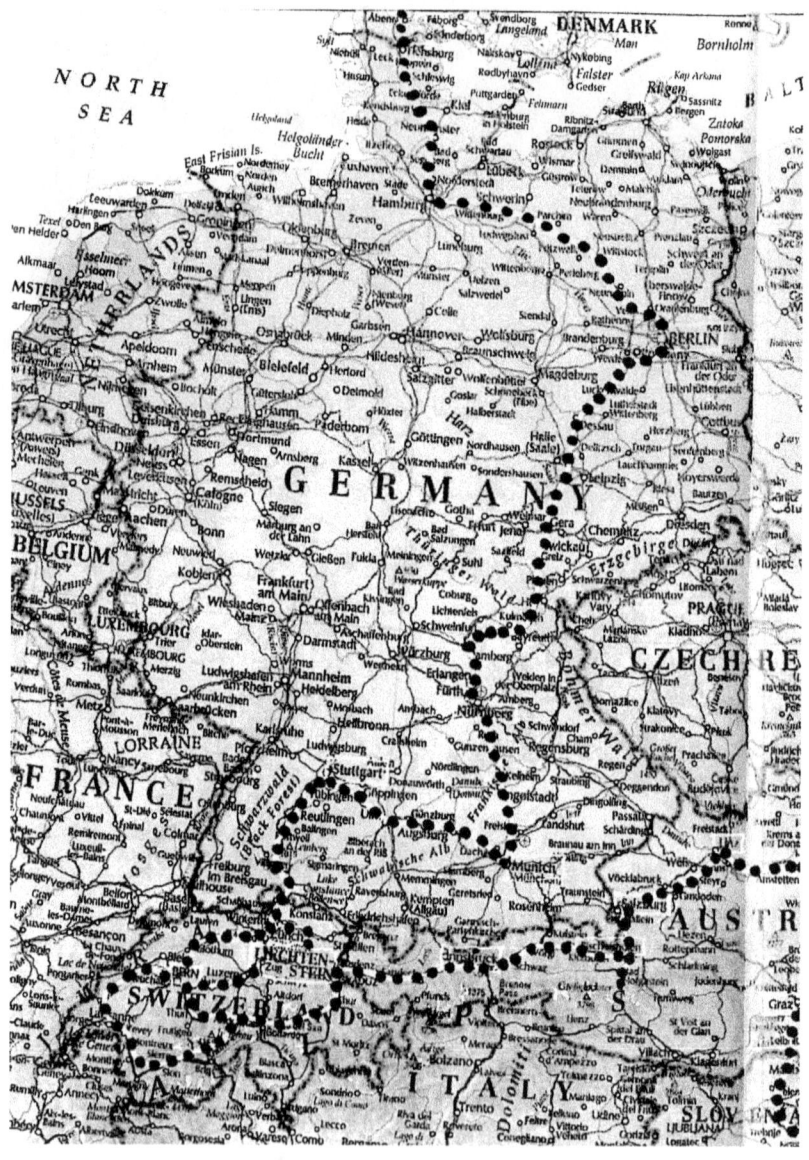

From Austria to Denmark

From Yugoslavia to Austria

Adriatic Coastline, Yugoslavia — Line of roadway high on left

Dubrovnik in Yugoslavia

CHAPTER THREE:

AUSTRIA

For the first time since being on the road, we had a problem with our international driving plate on the rear of Mirrabooka. It read AUS - the same as Austria. People were confused when we told them it was Australia ... and a lot of people didn't know where that was. Talking to them often turned into a geography lesson; in any case, it was always very interesting.

We rode into Gratz, where we cashed travellers cheques and, lashing out, bought ham and eggs for breakfast as a treat. Gratz turned out to be a very pretty city with beautiful old buildings. We parked 'Mirra' and explored on foot as there was so much to see. We had spent too much time in the outdoors and so, went and got lost in the museum and art gallery.

Then, leaving the city, we took a wrong turn and got lost again ... but were stopped by a Dane who asked about our AUS plate and, as a result, we had many cups of coffee while answering his questions about Australia. After that, we took a detour to some ski resorts and then, finally were on the road to Vienna: a good bitumen road with no pot-holes, loose gravel or washouts ... for a change.

***

We were cruising along nicely when two motorcycle policemen came upon us, one on each side as they escorted us for about three hundred yards. They then moved off, to be replaced by two police cars who pulled us over.

"Where are you going?" they asked.

"The camping place" we replied.

They said "Follow us."

So now there was one in front and one behind us. The blue blinking lights went on, then the sirens and the pace picked up. I was hoping they wouldn't stop in a hurry, because I didn't want to finish up on their bonnet ... they were pushing us.

We eventually came to what looked like a park – it was the camping place. It was huge – well laid-out, with masses of gardens. The police guided us to reception and booked us in. They apologised for hurrying us along but it was necessary, as we had been holding up traffic and had created a big traffic jam on the autobahn. People had been slowing down to get a good look at us and the end of the line was at a crawl, even though there were two and three lanes. We were now in civilised Europe and had been unaware of how we must have looked different from the locals!

The police reminded us to be careful on the autobahn and to keep in the slow lane. We thanked them for looking after us and then they were off.

The site we were given was close to the amenities block – I think they were telling us something. We put the tent up amidst a lot of onlookers. Then Keith went off to the very-large amenities block, while I looked after the camp and wrote up my diary. Keith came back all clean and polished ... then it was my turn. I was amazed at the size of the block and looking in the mirror, I could well see why we looked different – anyway, I too, came back well-polished.

* * *

The next five days we spent exploring. We visited the palace with its 405 grand rooms, gilded ceilings, sandalwood walls, inlaid floors and magnificent gardens. The main reason for being in Vienna at this stage was to get a visa for East Germany and Berlin – so, we found the East German embassy. It was in a bland-looking building with a sombre interior. The reception counter had two people behind it but behind that were two lines of interview rooms; one with glass fronts, the other all timber.

We asked about the visa and were given the usual stack of forms to fill in.

We made ourselves comfortable, leaning on the counter and filled them in. We got through them rather quickly, as we believed our reason for being here was very simple. We would be just passing through one of the corridors to Berlin and not staying in the country; but they wanted to know all the details of the reason for our visit to Berlin. Keith's niece being the reason, they wanted to know why she was there and how she got there. The answer was she had married a local ... and so it went on, until they gave up. They couldn't find anything and gave us our visas but tried to make us feel we had stolen something from them. What the visas did state was that we had twelve hours to get there from the border, which we brushed aside as not a problem.

That business being done, we went back to exploring. There was a huge park with music bowls scattered around, with various orchestras and lots of choirs. It was a case of take your lunch or dinner and find the one that suited, make yourself comfortable and drink it all in. The big orchestras would perform mainly in the big concert halls but some smaller ones would use the shells, along with the choirs. A whole day could be spent wandering around picking out the performances of choice. For us, after such an all-day session, we would go home at night with Mozart, Beethoven, Brahms, Schubert and Strauss ... and there wasn't much room in the tent after we all got in.

We were unable to see a live performance because we never had the proper attire to wear; but there was as always, an upside: we did get to ride on Vienna's trams, which were good for moving around the city. We walked to the city walls, where Genghis Kahn had called a halt to his invasion of Europe. The walls didn't stop him but the death of the Grand Kahn Ogodei did, in 1242. He was in Hungary, ready to invade Austria but retreated home. Apart from Genghis, Vienna had seen invasions by the Celts, Romans, Vandels, Visigoths, Huns, Avarps and Slavs, then finally, us ... we all came and went.

* * *

Being in Vienna, we continued to explore and had a close look at the Danube only to discover that the Blue Danube was not blue but brown and fast-flowing. The river was swollen from heavy rains up-stream and craft were securely tied to pylons. There was a large Russian cruise boat, the 'Odessa', which we were invited to have a look over and so, we went aboard. We were impressed with the boat but, looking at the mooring ropes straining against the current, we thought if the ropes were to break, we would have a quick trip to the Black Sea and never see the scooter again.

We visited the Vienna Woods taking our daypacks and enjoyed walking through the big forest. At lunchtime we found a picnic area with tables and seating, where we ate lunch. All was peaceful and quiet, until an elderly Austrian lady decided to join us and plonked herself down beside Keith ... then proceeded to tell him her life story.

Keith kept moving away from her but she kept close to him, then said, "I married some horrible men, some of them, cruel to me. They had no parents and had not been brought up proper." Then she started to paw at Keith who by now, was on his feet.

I picked up the packs and said to Keith, "It's time to do a runner." We moved off but she tried to hang onto him.

He finally broke away, then said to me, "Why do I attract old ladies and stray dogs?"

I said, "It might be your ginger beard – but look at it this way: we heard a tale, live from the Vienna Woods."

Keith's reply was, "Very funny."

We went back to ride the large 49 metre ferris-wheel there

which, from the top, gave us an excellent view over the city and the church spires; especially St Stephen's, which really stood out. Back on the ground, we had a good look at a museum and said "Good-day", to some friends – I was looking at the rear axle when Don, our American friend, turned up and gave me a hand. The axle was off-centre and four hands were better than two.

We then booked ourselves in for a tour of the back stage of the Opera House, which was most-inspiring. We looked at the props and scenery along with the machinery used to move it.

* * *

It was time to move on and to ride on the autobahn (in the slow lane), which gave us time to see the castles on the hilltops. We followed the Danube through Linz, then St Wolfgang. This was picture-postcard country, with lakes, boats, swans, mountains and quaint, thatched- and shingle-roofed houses – not to mention, the home for the musical White Horse Inn.

Riding through beautiful Salzburg, we were greeted by a hail storm with very large hail, which blocked the stormwater systems, leaving the city awash. We rode through and out the other side, to try and find a zimmer (guest house) for the night. We found one, opposite what was once Hitler's Berchtesgaden. We couldn't see much of it as the cloud was down.

Berchtesgaden is in the Bavarian Alps and Kehlstein, at 1834 metres, is a sheer-sided mountain which overlooked what had been Hitler's retreat, called 'Eagles Nest'; this was once complete with maze-like bunkers, built into the alpine rock.

We found our zimmer and settled in for the night as it was pouring outside. We had a hot dinner to warm ourselves up but when we got into our beds they were also, blazing hot. The building was heated and our beds had thick duvets on top. It was boiling with the heating on and cold, with it off; so we pulled out our sleeping bags – and that worked!

Next day, we paid the toll on the steep Brenner Pass where we stopped and went walking, to get some exercise. Through the pass to the glacier, the air was clear and the scenery magnificent. Then it was down to Heiligenblut, where the local band was playing to welcome us; along with the only campsite left in the camp-ground valley. At that we decided to return to Innsbruck – there were far too many people around. However, we did have views of the Dolomites across in Italy.

After obtaining another new tyre in Innsbruck, we donned our rucksacks and went walking some of the mountain tracks. After that, it was back onto the scooter and off to Liechtenstein, followed by Switzerland, where we took an alpine gravel road to

Oberalp, at 2410 metres. A long, downhill run followed through snow (I now had my fur gloves on) and then went up over the next pass, at 2774 metres. There we camped the night amongst the snow and stars, with thankfully, no wind. Daylight brought us magnificent views of the mountain peaks. We walked around a frozen lake and climbed the peak behind, where we had 360 degree views of the mountain mass, from the Matterhorn to Mont Blanc. We spent quite some time there, looking out and taking photos.

It was back on the scooter, for the lengthy descent through long, narrow gorges, tunnels, past waterfalls and then, Interlaken - a beautiful but expensive place.

A few times on the long downhill run, Keith said to me, "We are going a bit quick, aren't we?"

I thought so too but I didn't tell him that. All I said was "It's gravity."

We visited Bern and the alpine museum; then Luzerne, where we spent time by the lake, with its many sailing boats. Our rear wheel needed adjusting and we found a garage by the lake: a perfect spot; and we did need a brake adjustment. More than ever, we needed our brakes. They had looked after us pretty well but, if we didn't look after them, ... ?? After that, it was time to be off to Zurich, Stuttgart and Germany.

* * *

Things had promptly changed with post-war development and the rebuilding of the damage. We stopped at the Rhine Falls and looked at the hydro station, then went on to the Black Forest and Lorrach ski resort. We were now in the tourist strip and so, on into Titisee, with its lovely lake where we met a character with two young, polar bears on leads. He wouldn't be doing that for much longer.

The rebuilding of Stuttgart was in top gear, with roads being rebuilt and buildings going up. The traffic flow on the autobahn seemed to be ninety percent trucks of all shapes and sizes – and moving quickly. We came to a massive truck stop with hundreds of trucks refuelling and with the drivers also, taking on fuel. On to Munchen, we continued and went straight to the camping platz, which was run by a South African.

He said, "No charges to you. I like the way you are travelling. If you need anything just ask." We thanked him.

We stopped at Raphael's (a famous shop), to watch the clock strike eleven and see the china figures move around every ten minutes. There were knights on chargers and dance figures, with a building backdrop of Munchen.

Lunch was in a beer cellar where, we found out later, Hitler used to hold meetings during his rise to power. It was amazing how the cellar survived the bombing. There was a Gothic style building nearby, which held the council chambers and we watched the council in session. Everything was in German but we could understand the basics of what was happening – politics sound the same everywhere!

The building was interesting with its carved ceilings and walls. From the tower, we could see three churches with tall, needle-like spires. A visit to the museum, which was huge, took in history, geography, boats, aircraft, cars etc. There were working models of mines and machinery ... and the list went on.

It was back onto 'Mirra' and off to Nuremberg via the autobahn, past wheat fields and pine forests, to arrive at our camping place, packed with scouts from France. We had just got our tent up, when a busload of Finns were dropped off.

The next morning, having cooked our porridge with our Yugoslavian fuel in our burner, we rode out to the stadium built by Hitler for the 1936 Olympic games. It too, had escaped the bombs but everything else around was in ruins. A mediaeval castle had also escaped the bombs and we paid a German-speaking guide there to show us over the stone castle, with narrow walkways, large rooms and mediaeval armour. It held a dank atmosphere. We looked at other buildings and places of interest and then set off to East Germany, arriving at the border where queues of people were waiting to be processed.

It was bedlam at the border. On the west side, there were customs and military police, both German and American; then there was a no-mans land. Next were East German customs, military police and Russian troops ... the cold war was still on.

(Keith had a niece, married to a German, who lived in West Berlin and she had invited us up, to visit and stay awhile.)

The plan was to take one of the traffic corridors through East Germany to Berlin. We had joined a queue to be processed and the movement was slow, because of the paperwork and searching through possessions. The Russians were making their presence felt, pushing people around.

A group of American military police I noticed, were talking to their Russian counterparts and looking at us. One of the Americans walked over to us and said, "I presume your papers are in order. I have spoken to the Russians, so we will process you over there and shorten the line."

The Americans, then the Russians, checked and stamped our papers and we were able to move on to the British sector. Before leaving, the Russians reminded us that the visa gave us twelve hours to get from where we were, into Berlin and no longer ... and that this was the last fuel stop.

* * *

We were now in East Germany and there was an immediate difference. All the buildings looked as though the war had ended yesterday. The road was full of pot-holes and damage was everywhere. Leipzig was our first town or city, looking gaunt and grey – but it did have a good roadside café. When the locals took a keen interest in us, we made sure we were on our best behaviour. There was a constant movement of police and the occasional Russian, along the road. We had a good meal and then set off.

I said to Keith, "We are not going to make our deadline – what with it being late and the hold up at the border ... and I don't fancy driving through these pot-holes in the dark. We could have a spill."

I suggested that we find somewhere to camp the night and take our chances at the border. Keith agreed. We hadn't gone far when we came to an unused barn, half-full of hay. There was no sign of settlement anywhere, so we moved in. We were at least comfortable and out of the weather.

We got away at daybreak and hadn't gone far when we had a flat tyre, which took a little while to fix. We then pushed on to the Russian zone, taking the damaged tyre with us as part of our excuse for being late. Berlin was at that time, divided into four zones: British, French, American and Russian – the Russian, being our exit point to get through to the British sector.

We were cruising along nicely, when I saw a blue flashing light in the rear-vision mirror. Ah! ... another police car moving fast – and this was not Vienna! We came to a screaming halt with the police car beside us ...

"Where have you been? You are late." First, passports were inspected, then visas, which were studied and then handed back – but fingers were pointing to the date and times on the visa. We were told to follow them and I did my best to keep up but they still had to slow down for us.

We stopped at the Russian/East German checkpoint and were descended upon by both police and army. We were taken away to a hut for interrogation while the police swarmed over Mirrabooka, taking all our gear off in order to examine everything. In the hut, we were seated at a table with four chairs – two for us and two for the police.

The questions came thick and fast, "Where have you been for these past ten hours?"

We spoke about being late from the border, how pot-holes made for slow travel and of our not wanting to travel over them in the dark. We had found a barn (and gave the location) and had to repair a tyre (and showed them the tyre). The questions just kept coming. After what seemed a long time, they up and left, closing the door.

Keith whispered to me, "I think this hut is bugged." We talked about the 'Rabbit' and cricket for over an hour. Finally, an officer came and said we could go. When we got down to Mirrabooka, our gear was all scattered around – they had been into everything. We packed in a hurry because we were now in their way. Everything had seemed to be in order.

We then rode on to the actual gate and were checked once again, crossed no-mans land and then checked into the British zone. We were now in Berlin.

Then I heard the sound of machine gun fire coming from where we had been. The noise was continuous. It had been a weapons firing- range, with small arms and machine guns. In all our time in Berlin we could hear it, on and off, twenty-four/seven. It seemed to be their way of saying, "We are here".

* * *

Keith had been given a phone number to ring when we arrived. He rang and was told a car would come and guide us to Charlottenburg, where Hans and Joachim Kopplin lived. The car arrived and we tailed him to Charlottenburg where we parked in front of Schoke Place, a quaint hotel, for lunch. We were invited to sit at a large table loaded with stacks of food. While we ate, there was a procession of visitors, come to meet us and also partake of the food. We talked and nibbled until 6 pm, when the scooter was put away in storage under a block of very modern flats. We were treated by everyone like royalty.

We collected our rucksacks and were taken by car to our unit, a short distance away. Our room was on the fifth floor of a new building with views out over the city. After a drive around the district, it was back home ... with a real bed and all mod-cons. We breakfasted in the unit, then were off to Schoke Place for lunch. In order to recover from lunch, we walked to the Australian mission to sign forms and get passes which allowed us to move around the city. We also collected our mail. At the mission, we were given afternoon tea – something we could well have done without. However, we fixed that by a brisk walk back to the pub for dinner.

It was late when we got back to our unit but we weren't there long before two VW beetles turned up ... they were going to take us for a drive. It was 11 pm and everyone piled in – five in each car. We drove around the city until 1 am, then had a meal. At 3 am we returned to our unit. Breakfast was at 10 am, lunch at 3 pm and dinner at 10 pm. I believe all this was a distraction for people living on an island, surrounded by barbed-wire. We had been the distraction!

The Berlin airlift had long finished when we arrived but corridors had been established, to get supplies and materials in and out of the city. We had come in on one of them, via the Russian zone. We walked around the retail area where there was plenty of activity and much money changing hands. We walked to British headquarters amongst the ruins, surrounded by high barbed-wire. The machine guns were still rattling in the background.

We got a lift into the Russian zone and to the Brandenburg Gate, which now looked like a Roman ruin except that it was still standing intact; but on its own, with desolation all around.

The Russians had a memorial built at right angles to the Gate, with details on a very large plaque - I presume about the conflict; I don't speak or read Russian.

The site was manned by six guards in full regalia, right down to their highly-polished jackboots. Four were on standby, whilst the other two strutted the length of the memorial, passing each other in the centre. While strutting, the heels of their boots rose over their heads. I thought they looked ridiculous; at the same time, I was amazed at how they kept their balance.

When we tired of their performance, we turned our attention to the Gate and the steps going up the columns to the walkway over the road. It was only then that we realised how big the Gate was - it was massive. Taking a photo from over the edge, I dropped my lens cap from the Praktica and it lodged in a crack somewhere above the road - where it probably still is - but at least it was resting back in the place of its origin.

* * *

The next three days, we spent with reporters and newsmen, who bought new tyres and film for us in return for our story and photos. They also passed us a handful of cash - I can't remember how much it was -but we were also given another handful after our TV interview two days later.

Keith bought flowers for our hosts, while I worked on the scooter. We had TV staff descend on our unit in order to set up for the following morning. The place was strewn with cables, flood lights and tripods. We had to be careful moving around as the unit wasn't large.

Next morning, it was action time. We were filmed eating breakfast, packing our rucksacks, going down to the scooter, loading up, saying goodbye and then, riding off into the distance. It was Take 1, Take 2 ... and so on. Going up and down the steps with our gear, loading and unloading the scooter - all this took up the whole morning. They finally packed up and left, passing us another lot of cash, telling us they had enjoyed themselves. We too, had enjoyed a lot of fun but we were pleased to see them go ... it had all been full-on.

What we weren't aware of at the time was that the whole thing had been screened all over Europe. We only found that out later when people began waving at us and bringing us food. The welcomes were like having another passport! This lasted for ten weeks and it was all very friendly and warming.

That evening after the TV interview, we were taken to a night club with two floors, two big bands and two large bars. We were dressed in the best we had - ie. what we were wearing -

except that we were now clean; we had even polished our boots and combed our beards. When we arrived, we were served a hearty meal of smoked eel and sausage.

The downstairs band was from Sweden but we were the feature of the night, being introduced as two travelling Australians from Down-Under. We looked the part with our beards and sun- bleached clothing. We were invited to sing and gave them a rousing rendition of Waltzing Matilda for which we received three encores.

We weren't drunk as most people thought we were – and as most people themselves were getting – we were in fact stone, cold sober.

The band struck up and we were invited to dance. Keith, never being one for dancing, smartly vanished. I didn't have to look for a partner – the girls were queueing up to have a dance with the big-footed one, from Down-Under. I found a lot of the girls couldn't much speak English but they certainly understood it ... and were a lively lot. The floor was packed, so all I could do was shuffle. A big, blonde-headed chap lent over and whispered in my ear, "You had better watch out. Some of the girls might like to migrate to Australia."

I said, "Thanks, I'll keep that in mind."

It seemed like hours on the floor, for the band seldom stopped. I was in a progressive barn-dance where you change partners, when I decided I had had enough. I slipped out, found Keith and we left the night club.

On the way out, we were presented with a huge bunch of flowers which we took home to give to Hans and Joachim; after a taxi ride at 4 am, we arrived to find two German plain-clothes police checking us in – but all very polite.

The next morning, we gave Hans and Joachim the enormous bunch of flowers which we had received at the night club. We chattered on and finally told them how we had been checked-in by two plain-clothes policemen.

Hans smiled and said, "You know, you two have been under surveillance ever since you arrived in Berlin via East Germany and they have also known that you had a 'short' interview with the East German police; but it appears that nothing came of it."

Keith looked at me and said, "In India, we were picked-up as possible Russian spies ... and we haven't even finished our trip yet!"

Next day passed as a time to recover; then we packed for real the following morning and reluctantly, said goodbye to everybody. We had had a humbling experience and thanked everyone concerned. The farewells took some time but finally we rode off into the distance, for a final take.

Then it was back to reality and into East Germany; with more Russian police, filling in more forms and again, passports to be checked and stamped. When we got to the West German border, we had to do it all over again. It was now raining and we rode straight through to Hannover; then on to Hamburg in pouring rain. We found a shelter shed in a pine forest and managed to sleep a dry night on peat moss.

* * *

The Alps at Innsbruck, Austria

Mirrabooka at The Brandenburg Gate, Berlin

Russian War Memorial adjacent Brandenburg Gate, East Berlin

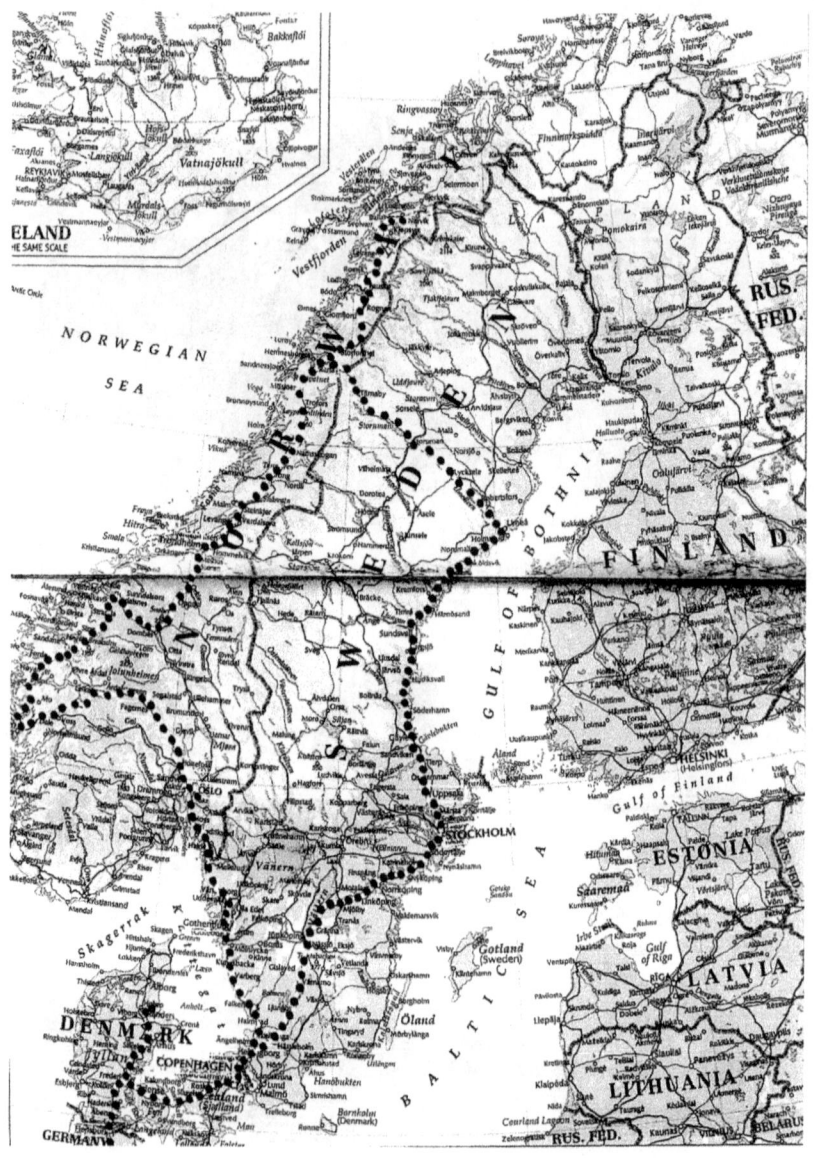

From Denmark, North and Back

The border between Germany and Denmark was at Flensburg, on a fjord where we passed through customs. The harbour was busy with ferries of all sizes from passenger, to car, to truck and to heavy equipment. We went straight up the east coast to Randers at the top of the peninsula, travelling over undulating farm country.

Along the way, we were riding through heavy rain on a long, straight stretch of road, when a car pulled along side and indicated for us to stop. We pulled over and the driver of the car got out in the rain and in perfect English said, "The rain is very heavy. Let me take your wife in the car. She will get drowned."

Keith, sitting behind me, pulled down the scarf which covered his face, displaying his ginger beard. The drivers mouth fell open and he said, "Sorry," climbed back in the car and drove off at speed.

We were travelling to Randers to meet a friend, whom we had met in Austria. Peter was a mechanic and we had been invited to his farm to meet the family. When we arrived, we were greeted like long-lost family. After dinner, we had a good sing around the piano; then we were off to our bedroom in the hayloft beside some rabbits and pigs, brought in out of the rain. We all slept well, including the pigs!

Next morning, it was still raining but after a yoghurt and rye bread breakfast, we retraced our steps to Copenhagen, where we went to the Australian consulate to collect mail and check the weather forecasts for Norway and Sweden. We were told that Norway was going to have its wettest season in 100 years and Sweden, not much better. It looked as though we were going to have rain all the way to the Cape.

We were discussing whether to give Norway a miss and go to Spain, when the sky cleared and brilliant sunshine burst forth to light up the landscape. We had been on the road too long and now we were listening to the weather gods ... and they said, "Come forth to Norway." So, we packed supplies and went forth, ... crossing the border at Gothenburg, where we camped in a Norwegian pine forest.

Next morning, on our way to Oslo, we were given another breakfast at a road side café, courtesy of our earlier TV interview. This treat brought the number of these impromptu breakfasts to five ... and all were thankfully received.

At this point we climbed over a mountain range, when the rain started again and steep mountains became waterfalls. The wild, rugged scenery, with its 2000 metre high peaks, ran up along the west coast making for spectacular scenery; even though it was wet but impossible for photos. We would be riding on steep, winding roads and occasionally a shaft of sunlight would burst through the gloom to light up the magnificent scenery. I would stop for a photo and it would close over again.

The trolls did not like me ... or possibly, it was my camera!

* * *

We had bridges to cross over inlets and an occasional ferry ride. Parts of the country were covered in yellow wildflowers and then the snow started, making the picture even better. Rivers turned into lakes, which had wonderful reflections and housed salmon hatcheries, which would feed on mosquitos.

We found the camping place, booked in and were given a site beside some Danes, Brits and Dutch campers; all of whom loved to sing, especially when the sun went down. That was when the dancing started. It was mainly folk dances but being on the grass, it made for lots of fun, including when the English and Dutch became competitive. We had four nights at this campsite and it was on, every night. The nice part about it was that other groups became involved; so it never kept anyone awake.

For us, every new day held something different. One day, it would be the Royal Palace, which we found very different from the others we had visited; not as lavish but lovely nevertheless. On another day, it was to be the Viking museum, which kept us entertained with its long boats, timber crafts and housing.

We visited the Royal Palace, the Tiki folk museum and the Viking ships displays – which I found most interesting, having heard and read so much about them. I spent a lot of time looking at their construction.

I was especially-interested in this, as my mother's father had come from here and was a carpenter and a house-builder back in Australia. I inherited his huge tool box, full of his wood-working tools, including the broad-axes they used to split logs and dress them. Those same axes, hundreds of years earlier, were used to build long-boats and then later, were used for splitting heads.

We moved on to the explorer ships, 'Fram' and 'Kon-Tiki'. We spent a lot of time in the folk museum, which also covered national dress and the ways of living over the centuries. Log cabins and multi-storied log cabins with turf roofs, for both insulation as well as for grazing sheep and goats to keep the grass short.

All the clothes were brightly-coloured, with red being the favourite colour. One museum we visited, took in Africa, Asia and America ... and even Australia.

The Oslo camping ground was an absolute league of nations. We had two Americans and a Dane, Hendrick by name, close-by and we would all talk until 2 am.

* * *

On the road to Lake Tryvann, pine logs were being harvested and rafted down the river to the sawmills. The country was quite a picture, with waterfalls flowing into the lakes. From there it was on to Hønefoss, a big town, with a model of a giant long-boat in the main street; and again, on to Brandou where we camped in the pine forest, with wild flowers, running-creek and mosquitos – where we had to make a smoking fire to keep them away. A group of people turned up at 11 pm and had oom-pa-pa band practice ... trumpets, trombones, tubas etc, all very entertaining but the mosquitos eventually won; and so, the truck drove off, with the band on the back, oom-pa-paring into the night and taking their mosquitos with them.

The next day, we rode through to Fagernes in pouring rain. It was even so, a very pretty drive, following rivers and lakes. Then at Maristua, we were amongst the snow and walked to a large waterfall, where steel ladders were bolted to the rock face, allowing us to climb up and down the waterfall.

There were many tunnels along the way, to avoid snow drifts. At Sognefjorden, we had our first fjord ferry ride to get to the other side, followed by bridges – all very spectacular. It was a good ferry ride, to finish up with freshly-cooked salmon beside the light house at 11 pm. We had greasy roads next day as we followed the rivers and lakes towards Lom, having to pull off the road several times because of heavy rain and fast-flowing streams.

Next day, the sun came out briefly and we had a chance to dry off. On reaching Otta, the road became worse because of the rain. There were caution signs all along the way, with numbers 1,2,3 and so on. Number 1 took us onto a high, heath plateau with a long climb up past Mt Galdhøpiggen. At 2468 metres, it was very cold, with snow falling. The scenery was wild and rugged with countless waterfalls, while the road was greasy. We were heading towards Lom, when we were forced to pull over because of the volume of water ... but it was spectacular. We actually found a day-loggers' camp and settled in for the night.

At Drivusta railway station, we took a break to admire the view across the valley filled with lots of hay-drying racks. Dombas was a food supply stop and while we couldn't carry much, we had to stock up in case we got stranded. The store was a typical country store, which not only sold food but also hardware supplies, rakes, shovels, snow shoes, skis, paint and plumbing supplies.

* * *

Suddenly, the landscape changed as we got away from the big mountains. We were now travelling along the Trondheim fjord and behold – a bitumen road – what a luxury! In Trondheim, we found there was a camping place in the racecourse, with all amenities – wow! The sun didn't set until 11 pm, so we had daylight to settle in.

From Trondheim, we took the road to Hell ... I took a wrong turn and had to stop to ask a passer-by, if this was the road to Hell. The passer-by turned out to be an American officer assigned to NATO but dressed in civvies. When I asked the question, I was greeted with a roar of laughter and an American voice replied, "I have been on that one and it's not here ... but there is another road to Hell, just over there." We all had a good laugh. From Hell, the road followed the Trondheim fjord into farming country. We passed through some big, modern towns to Steinkjer, with the rain following us but we were lucky, when we found a number of open barns, in which we took shelter.

Next, we had the long run to Mosjøen country, now starting to look like tundra, having many lakes with numerous small islands in them, covered with pine and a thick vegetation of ferns and mosses – it looked something like the south of Tasmania; lots of big, fast-flowing rivers, being used to transport large logs down to sawmills.

On reaching a cairn beside the road to mark the Arctic Circle, we were surprised to see a railway line nearby and pointing north. Looking at the lines, they didn't appear to be at all well-used.

We were getting cold, so to warm up, we climbed a peak with a glacier on one side and where the scenery was breathtakingly beautiful.

Mosjøen was a large timber town, with houses scattered around the landscape. Moving north, we were in flat, swampy country with mosses growing in huge clumps about two feet thick; then on to Mo I Rana, a coal and timber town, which held polar celebrations early August but we were too late for them. The masses of mosquitos, which at times descended on us, reminded us of the RAF timber-frame, mosquito fighter-bombers of the Pathfinder Squadron, which had marked the drop-zone for the bombers with tins of red paint on the snow-covered plateau where the Nazis were working on the heavy-water programme to make atom bombs. The result from the Pathfinders effort and the bombing, stopped the project.

Also in those years, the Norwegian Partisan fighters had managed to wear down the invading forces, who were trying to find them and stop their activity. It was a long battle and I believe the Nazis were worn-out.

* * *

We decided to see how far north we could get towards Narvik. We were warned that if the weather was too bad, the ferries might not run; and to get to Narvik, we had six ferry-crossings. We almost got there but, coming out of a tunnel, we were greeted by a hail storm with very large hail, some the size of cricket balls. I did a very quick u-turn back into the tunnel to take shelter from the bombardment. It was the biggest hail I had ever seen. If we had got caught out in that, we would have been pulverised. It lasted for about twenty minutes but felt like hours. We now felt that we had been told to go no further. Under the conditions, we had had a good run and what lay ahead would have been a repeat of what we had already seen.

We retraced our steps to Mo I Rana, where we had stopped in a "B and B" the night before and, on parking the scooter under cover, were greeted by the owner with, "I have been expecting you. How far did you get?"

We told him and he said, "I have been talking on the phone to Narvik and they told me the weather has closed right in and visibility is almost zero." We had made the right decision. Now, we had a proper building with fireplace, a hot dinner and a warm bed ... and no mosquitos!

Bacon and eggs were for breakfast; then we loaded up and were off to Sweden. The road was a windy one through the forest, where we said, "Goodbye" to the mountains and arrived at the border checkpoint. We were now on the long, downhill run off the mountains. The waterfalls gradually decreased and the lower we got, the more swampy it became.

At Storuman, we were back into logging country with sawmills and timber jinkers, which for us were a menace, as they would take up the whole road; and to them, two blokes on a motor scooter looked like a speck on the landscape. On one occasion, I saw one coming and got over as far as I could to let him pass but he only got half his length past us when he moved over, almost putting us under the jinker. That didn't worry me as much as the rear wheels of the jinker, which seemed to be lining up with the scooter.

I screamed out to Keith, "Hang on, we're going over into the bog."

The road was flat and at the same level as the bog. Over we went and were pleasantly surprised to find we were on a giant mattress of moss. As we hit the moss, the rear wheels screamed past us. They would have only needed to clip us and we would have gone over anyway. Doing it this way, we had some control over our fall. We were both in one piece and still sitting on the scooter but slowly sinking into the moss, which brought us back to reality. We had to take everything off the scooter, including us, then drag the machine back to the road, which wasn't far away.

When the scooter was back on the road, we spoke for the first time – and it was brief, "That was close."

* * *

It was late in the day, when we reached Lycksele and found a beautiful place to camp, with fireplace and wood supplied. We had our dinner and we were preparing to retreat into the tent, when swarms of mosquitos descended on us. Thankfully, we had sealed the outside of the tent with earth and we scrambled inside, zipping up the door. It was full on, with mosquitos belting on the tent to try and get at us. It was just like heavy rain falling on the tent and the noise was like a formula-one race track, with the cars screaming around the outside – millions of them. This kept up all night. It seemed as if we were the only available source of blood and we didn't know where else they had been, before they arrived here. We gave up talking, as we had to shout at each other. Fortunately, it was cold enough to make us want to burrow into our sleeping bags and close our hoods.

A little after daybreak, all was quiet. They seemed to have gone but we waited a little longer just to make sure. When we finally emerged, they had all gone. My diary note read, 'Mosquitos! VERY BAD NIGHT – not good'.

After that, we thought we should head for the coast, away from forests. The road to Umea was a construction site with dams and hydro stations being built, along with new roads and new towns/cities.

All along the way, we were recognised as the two on the TV interview in Berlin and we would be flagged down, taken to road side cafes, fed and watered. We finally reached the coast and stopped at a pretty little beach near Sundsvall. We were now in an industrial area at Hudiksvall. The rain caught up with us again, lasting until Soderhamn, where we camped ... and we were still being fed and watered.

* * *

We travelled south through pine forests, cities and gardens to Uppsala; through rain all the way and found another sawmill for shelter. We now arrived in Stockholm in brilliant sunshine. Moving around the city, we were still being recognised and so were enjoying a very-cheap visit to Stockholm. We made a regal entry into the camping ground and were given the royal treatment ... but it was ironic that we had all this attention whilst having the smallest tent in the campground. We were told, "No charges," on anything and we were kept busy signing autographs. We were very impressed by the coverage which we had been given by that interview.

We were given a guide to show us around and visit museums, Lapp displays and the Tivoli Gardens, with its live entertainment, including half-hour vaudeville shows and orchestras playing around the park and music in all forms.

We visited the 'Vandarum': a well-preserved sailing ship, now converted into a youth hostel and looking very dignified, all dressed in white.

Outside Stockholm, we stopped to admire a large timber home with a turf roof ... and the name across the front was, 'Wards Ouse'. I wondered if that had any connection to my name, for I certainly would not have minded the house.

Then, the rain started again as we set off to Denmark. It was beautiful farming country and we called in on Lars and his wife, whom we had met in Dubrovnik; where they had invited us to call when we were in Denmark. We were asked to stay for a while to catch up. It was a good visit and we said our goodbyes, setting off to the campground in Copenhagen.

We got there ... but only just, as the coil and regulator went dead. As it turned out, Hans, whom we had met the night before, worked for Lucas, the electrical people; he had given us his card in case we needed anything ... and now we did. We rang him and told him of our problem, whereupon he despatched two replacements for us, which we received almost immediately. We fitted them and we were again mobile.

After looking in at the campground (again at no charge), we rode to the Consulate to collect any mail – and we had quite a bundle, including a letter from Fuji, letting us know that they had seen our TV interview and wished us well.

* * *

The Tivoli Gardens, Danish-style (as opposed to the Swedish-), had a strong Hans Christian Andersen theme. The Copenhagen gardens were similar, with a ferris wheel and side shows but had Hans Christian Andersen pantomimes with wonderful lighting. We were just starting to enjoy ourselves when the rain came down again, making us retreat to our camp site, where we remained for the next two days. However, the time was broken-up visiting other campers and being invited to sing-songs, which lasted until around midnight.

Eventually, the rain stopped and we visited The Little Mermaid, only to be surprised at how small she was.

We were on the road again, via Flensburg, to Hamburg. Being a port city, there were lots and lots of trucks, which blocked our view of street signs ... and when you are on a motor scooter at ground level in a canyon of trucks, it is very difficult to find your way. We finally got to the autobahn and so, on to Bremen with another maze. That day, we covered 602 kilometres and had two punctures.

Starting the scooter next morning, the muffler fell off, making a hell of a noise. It looked as if we were slowly disintegrating. I picked up the muffler and strapped it onto our baggage. Now we had to locate someone to weld it back on, as we had no means of doing so ourselves.

Sognefjorden Fiord, near Laerdaleora, around mid – Norway

Wards Ouse, Helingsborg, Sweden

The Square-rigger, 'Vandrararhem', used as a Youth Hostel, Stockholm, Sweden

Hans Christian Andersen's 'Little Mermaid', Copenhagen Foreshore

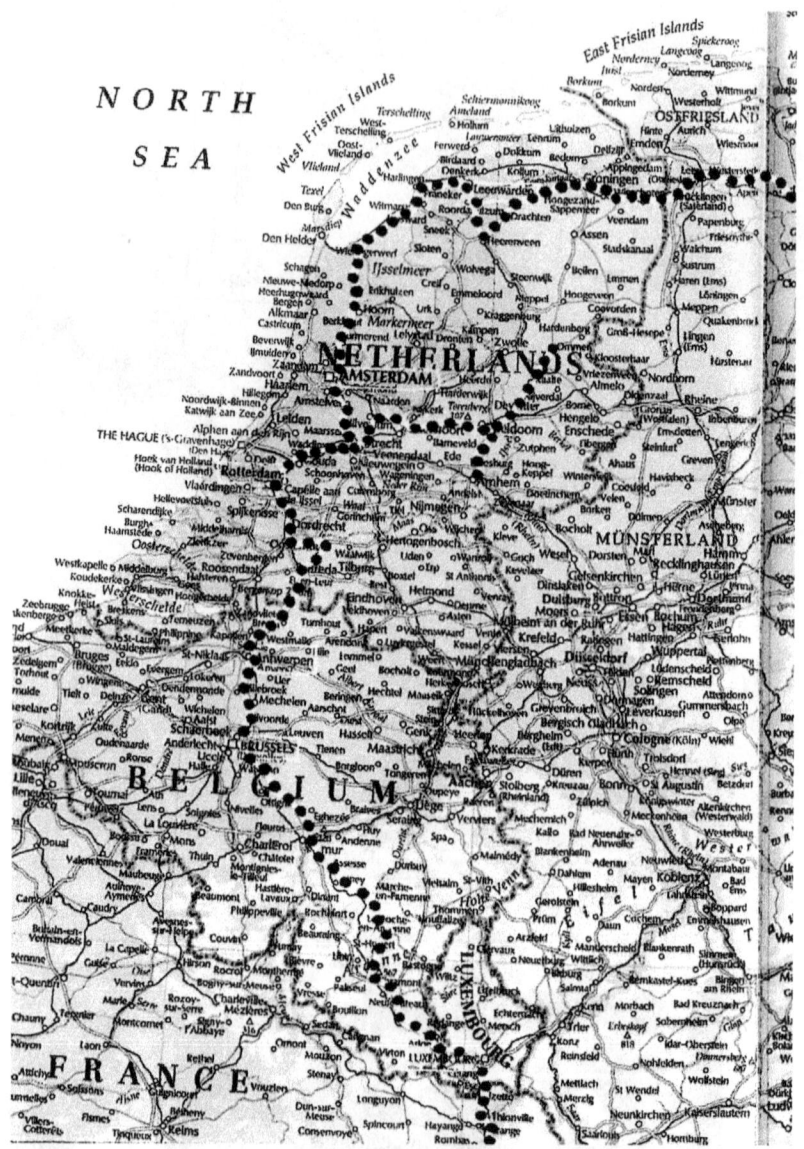

Holland & Belgium

SCOOTER NOMADS : BOOK TWO

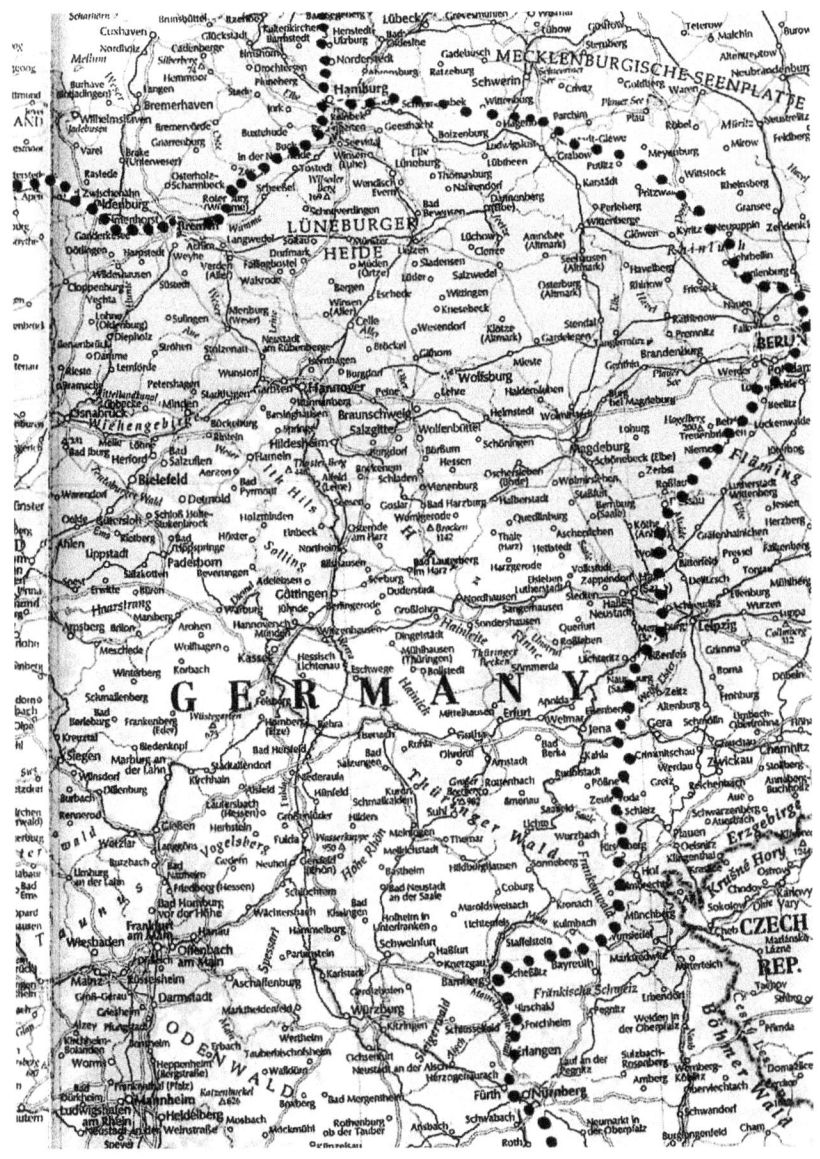

Through Germany to Denmark & back to Holland

Canal with barges, Amsterdam, Holland

Windmills at Kinderdijk, southern Holland

CHAPTER FOUR:

HOLLAND

We decided to make a run for Amsterdam, where Keith (having been there before) had friends who had invited us to visit and stay a while ... so, to Amsterdam it was. We rode in light rain on to Leeuwarden, which put us firmly in Holland, a colourful country. We took the dyke road across the massive dyke barrier built in 1934 to close off the bay from the sea and to join the two headlands with reclaimed land: now pasture, with cattle and sheep grazing. At the time of our visit, other dykes were either being finished or under construction.

Then the rain started again but the road was magnificent, especially the one on the inside of the dyke. At intervals along the wall, there were huge gates to allow ships through to Amsterdam. We arrived there at 5 pm in the pouring rain. How we ever managed to find the house is a mystery.

We were met by a man named Logke, who smoked a cigar and was very hospitable; he was the keeper of the house while the owners were at work. The owners were called Puck and Hemmi, who were related to another of Keith's sisters (Keith did have a large extended family). This of course, meant yet another late night.

After a Dutch breakfast of rye bread, we rode the scooter to the city and had the muffler fixed. While this was being done, we took a launch ride along the canals and the harbour; and learnt that the canals were ten feet deep, well-used by barges carrying coal to the city; in their creation, the mud from the canals was used for filling behind the dykes, to reclaim the land.

The buildings along the canals were something that had to be seen to be believed. Apart from their colourful façades, it was their structure, standing at odd angles due to subsidence, that was remarkable. Actually, they looked rather quaint: like dolls' houses but I wondered if the doors and windows could all open and shut. We left the launch and walked the narrow cobblestone streets and alleyways, passing these quaint buildings. We saw an organ grinder and his monkey performing; then spent a little time admiring a fourteenth-century timber church. We were there for over an hour and were fortunate that the tourists hadn't yet arrived.

We walked back home to a Dutch baked dinner, complete with vegetables - a real treat. After dinner, we crammed into Hemmi's car: a Citroën 2CV (or 'the ugly duckling', as they called it) ... but it was the only car for the narrow, cobblestone streets.

* * *

The road to Marken was over reclaimed dyke-country and was rough, pot-holed and closed-in by eight-foot-high reeds growing on either side of the road.

Along the coast, were fishing villages which had become isolated because of the marshes, which made them closed communities with a lot of inter-marrying. With the dykes, came better roads and more visitors but the villagers kept up their traditional form of life, with colourful dress, black caps and black, baggy pants for the men and white, pointy caps for the women, along with clogs. Marken was an all-timber village and the buildings appeared to blend in with the people.

Monnickendam, was another interesting village but this one was all built in brick, which didn't seem to be working too well, as subsidence was setting the buildings at odd angles and some were even toppling over. In the centre of the village was 'punishment square', with the original stocks still standing, inviting anyone to put his or her head and arms into the waiting holes. The hinged top-rail could be lowered, locking-in their head and arms, making them immobile. It was in those past times, that onlookers could then throw rotten fruit at the locked-in head. This remained a mediaeval form of torture up until the

Nineteenth Century. The suggestion we heard, was that it should perhaps be brought back for some people!

We were taken to a restaurant with atmosphere, candle-light and full of antiques, some for sale. I was able to have a good look at their mechanical whistling birds, which made the place sound like an aviary ... lots of places we visited in Holland had these novelties, in all shapes and sizes. We eventually had dinner, then drove back to the city in the light of a full moon. It had been a lovely evening.

At 8.oo am, we set off to visit Holland's Reebok National Park: a very beautiful part of the country with white sand-hills – one, being over three metres high – and clothed with pine trees, oak and berk (which looked like our paperbarks). Good walking-tracks led through the heather in full-bloom. Within the park were several small lakes with flat-bottomed boats, hired out by fishermen. It took us four hours to do the circuit. There was almost no bird life but we did see two foxes, rabbits, some domestic pigs gone wild, deer and squirrels.

* * *

Later that day, we retraced our steps to Amsterdam. It was a Sunday afternoon and everybody in the country who owned a pushbike, appeared to be out on the road ... there seemed to be thousands of them. We were with Hemmi and Puck in the 2CV and it took a lot of patience and time, to weave through the mass of humanity ... the bikes naturally, had right-of-way. How we missed our scooter!

We had time to take in the reflections in the canals, the beautiful sunset and a mist creeping through it. Next morning, after a rye breakfast (or rather, rye sandwiches filled with all sorts of things), we were off again in the 2CV beside canals and along by-ways on gravelled, reeded side-roads, to Gouda and its markets selling everything from fish to peanuts.

Taking the laneways and canals, we arrived in Rotterdam, the worlds second largest port and now, a very modern city, having been rebuilt after the war. We could not miss the flowers on sale in the shops – there were masses of them in a riot of colour.

Now we were travelling southeast on the N96 and to Kinderdijk ... where there were nineteen operating windmills, complete with tourists. Crossing the Waal and Maas rivers by ferry, we came to a pretty little town and camping place at Ridderkerk. We pitched our tents to the tune of the local band and dined at 9.30 pm.

The next day we rode to Edam and then, Volendam: another untouched village. The locals were still wearing national dress and looking very colourful. The men were in black baggy pants and clogs; the women had white pointed hats, multi-coloured dresses, aprons and again, clogs. Half the women had their hair plaited into short tails and with their starched aprons, looked very different.

We were at the wharf where the fishing fleet came in. There were a lot of inns on the waterfront and they were full of fishermen with their families. The fleet had arrived the previous evening and they had been celebrating all night. It was now mid-morning and they were still at it – singing, dancing and drinking.

We now continued back to Marken, in order to look at it in daylight; except that now, the tourists were around. It was washday and clothes and sheets were hanging everywhere. All of this would disappear, when the dyke was finally finished. The houses were all of timber and it looked like a Seventeenth Century pirate waterfront, as it had been isolated until the 1950's.

* * *

From here, it was back to Amsterdam to clean up our flat, ready for our departure in two days' time. That afternoon we drove to Bloemendaal, on the shore of the English Channel and with a beautiful beach. There were some people trying to swim in twelve inches of water – the tide was out. We sat and watched the sun, now a big red orb, sink slowly into the English channel and the following twilight.

The next day, we prepared for our departure by visiting friends we had made; as well as having people calling on us. The following morning we loaded the scooter, said our farewells and rode out, on to Belgium. We had had a wonderful time in Holland and it made us wish that we had spent some more time in other places also but it wasn't to be.

As we crossed the border into Belgium, there was only one thing the authorities were interested in: our insurance papers ... nothing else. We were all in the clear. It seemed to us that we had entered on the up-market side of the country: with big polished houses, with thick thatched roofs and immaculate and colourful gardens.

We continued on to Antwerp, the second city and the port for Belgium. This was a place of beautiful old buildings but for the intrusion of a huge supermarket: the first we had ever seen and it looked out of place in the surrounding settings. Streets were lined with trees for outdoor dining and all was softened with lots of flower beds. As it was getting late, we joined the diners on the footpath and had a lovely meal with orchestral accompaniment.

We rode on through the big industrial centres and camped

outside Brussels in yet another campground.

We awoke to a thick, pea-soup fog and had to wait until it lifted a little, before joining the fast-flowing traffic. The way was lined with flower beds, statues, and Gothic churches.

Then it was on to Liege: an attractive place, with big gardens and very hilly. We stopped at a place called Spa, which did have a spa and a spa-water health clinic. We camped at St Vith and then rode through beautiful hilly country, where harvesting had just finished. We continued now through to Luxembourg, where we bought some stamps and then, it was off to France.

Locals in national dress, Volendam, Holland

Thatched-roof house outside Brussels, Belgium

Street scene in Brussels, Belgium

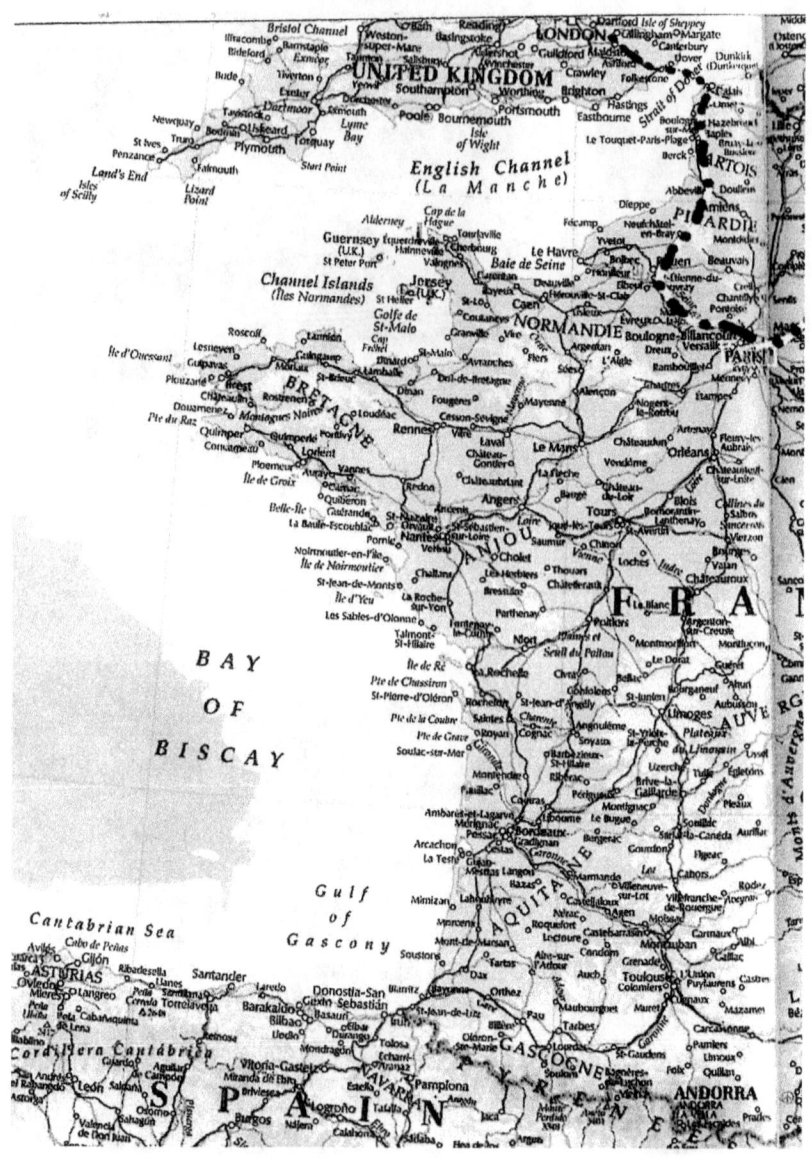

France: From Paris to Dover... Sans Mirrabooka

Belgium to France ... Paris & the end of 'Mirra'

'Mirrabooka' and local gendarme, Luxembourg

Paris and the Seine from the Eiffel Tower, Paris, France

CHAPTER FIVE:

FRANCE

We rode through big industrial towns and the city of Metz. We were now on the road to Verdun, having decided to get off the autobahn and stay in the country, where the traffic was slower and the scenery tranquil.

It was then, that the scooter started playing up. We were 280 kilometres from Paris. The country was beautiful: undulating green pastures with farm buildings scattered around ... it was a picture-postcard, rural scene with a blue sky. Then a loud rattle and a bang ... and the scooter stopped.

I examined the motor and found the piston had cracked. After 38,625 kilometres, it had finally happened. Poor old Mirrabooka, with all her problems, had hung in there with us and not once, left us stranded in a place where repairs could not be made ... and there had been a number of them. With the help of other people, 'Mirra' had always been fixed and we were on the road again.

The 200cc fluid drive motor was a big motor at that time and was regarded as a touring machine. It had 240 kilogram carrying capacity - Keith and I, plus gear, were well under that.

The 'Rabbit' had done well. The other feature it had, was an air-spring on the back wheel, which we could pump up according to the load.

Back in reality, we were 280 kilometres from Paris – and so, it was out with the map. We had kept away from the main road, for ease of travel and had not seen any traffic on this good road since we started. Keith suggested the railway. Right ... there was a rail line 14 kilometres away, running through a village, with the railway continuing through to Paris. So a plan was formed. We would push and ride 14 kilometres to the station, put ourselves and the scooter, on a train for Paris. 'We decided to give it a go.'

We had a good undulating road and a clear blue sky with beautiful rural scenery: perfect conditions ... and no traffic.

We would push the scooter up the hills, ride it down the other side and then, lying low on the handlebars, we could get half-way or better, up the next hill. We had covered 4 kilometres and it was getting dark.

We were passing a farmhouse when a curious farmer asked, "What are you doing?" We told him our story and he said, "You had better stop the night in the barn and get an early start in the morning." With our broken French, we thanked him and moved into his barn, which turned out to be deluxe, at least six stars – and we didn't have to share it with pigs.

* * *

We ate and slept well and woke ready for the task ahead. After our porridge breakfast and farewells to the farmer, we pushed off on the 10 kilometre journey. The system worked well and our fitness probably helped. As the day wore on and with the heat building up, we were in a lather of sweat and grime. We found out later, that that particular day had been the hottest in that part of France for 100 years. That sounded familiar – it's always either too hot, too cold or too wet ... although it was we this time, who were wet with sweat.

While taking a rest at the top of a hill and studying the terrain with the map, we concluded that we were travelling over a World War I battlefield – everything lined up with hills, valleys and trenches. We knew that, towards the end of the war, the front line was only 64 kilometres from Paris and to the north of where we were. One story we had heard, was that the French were then sending reinforcements to the front by taxi cabs ... since there had been a major traffic jam of truck transport on the roads, a bright French general decided this was the only way he could get his troops to the front. He engaged all of the Paris taxis to carry the troops and so, won the day. With our quiet road, the traffic was leaving us in peace; and peace for what might lay under the surface.

We pushed on and eventually, a town appeared a few kilometres away. We were saturated when we rolled into the main street and the railway station. The place seemed deserted. It was about 1.00 pm on a Saturday afternoon: siesta time. We parked 'Mirra' and Keith kept guard while I went for a walk, to try and find someone.

I hadn't got far, when I met a well-dressed gentleman walking towards me. We established that he spoke accented English and I spoke no French. I told him of our situation and he said, "Nothing happens on Saturday. Everyone has the day off."

With further conversation, I discovered that he was the station master, the mayor, the bank manager and also owned several businesses in town. I had hit the jackpot.

Right, first the train ... "Is there a train today to Paris?"

The reply ... "No, no train."

"Are you sure?"

Station master ... "I can check up at the station."

The station master spent half an hour on the phone, then said, "No regular trains but there will be a troop train, coming through from Berlin, in about two hours. I will get you on it. I will talk to the CO."

Then I told him we had no French francs but we did have travellers cheques. The bank manager then spoke up, "Come with me to the bank. I will cash some for you."

We left Keith with the scooter again and went to the bank. With French francs, I walked back to the station with the bank manager and bought our tickets, from the station master.

Then I asked him if he knew of a camping place in Paris. The station master replied, "As mayor of this town, I have that information." The mayor gave me a map, marking railways etc and a large camping place, on the banks of the Seine River.

He went on to explain, "When you arrive in Paris, you will have to change platforms to the underground. Take this train to the end of the line, then walk three kilometres, to the camping place." He said to leave the scooter at the station and he would book it through to London for us by rail and ferry. We paid up, the booking was made and he added that the railway would hold the scooter in Paris for us for a few days while we had a look around the city.

We stripped Mirrabooka of our possessions. We now had a rucksack each with what rations we had, tent and sleeping gear. Keith had his machete, which he was reluctant to part with. It had been most useful on any number of occasions, from building a cooking fire, digging trenches around the tent to stop flooding and opening the occasional tin can. This then, went into the tent roll. We thanked the station master, the bank manager and the mayor for all of 'his' help.

We hadn't long to wait before the train thundered into the platform. The scooter was whisked away to the goods van and loaded. Keith and I carried our loads to the open door and moved into a crowded carriage full of French paratroopers.

We were greeted by stoney faces and neither of us eyeballed them. They probably were unhappy about the train stopping to pick us up. On entering the carriage, a passageway was cleared for us and we were given a wide berth ... as apart from our looks, we probably didn't smell the best either. Other than that from the rattle of the train, there was no noise – all was quiet.

* * *

After what seemed like hours, we arrived in Paris and rumbled into the station. The doors opened and we were allowed to go first. On the platform, we got our bearings and followed the signs to the Metro. Yes, it was Saturday night in Paris and there were people everywhere. Lots of them were all dressed up, as though they were going to the theatre or some other formal event. As we walked, a passageway was cleared for us. We didn't look around but just kept walking steadfastly to our platform.

On checking the Metro line, we found that we had only minutes to wait for our train. Keith decided to rest his arm carrying the tent roll and, whilst lowering it to the ground, the machete fell out onto the platform; (I should point out, that at that time, Algerian terrorists were active in France and so it was not a good time to drop a machete onto a crowded platform, especially dressed and unkempt as we were). The crowd moved away from us, leaving us as an island in their midst. Keith smartly shoved the machete back into the tent roll.

Then we heard a blast from a police whistle. We did not know who the blast was for but when you think you are guilty, you do your best to endeavour to act normal. There were more whistle blasts along the platform and people were all starting to move around as we saw Gendarmes' caps moving through the crowd.

We looked at each other and said, "Is that for us or someone else?"

At that moment, the train roared into the platform. Doors flew open and passengers alighted in a rush from the open doors. Once they had cleared, it was our turn. Because of our bulk, we were allowed to go first. Diving into the carriage, we took up an out-of-the-way position. The doors slammed shut and we were off, like a cork out of a bottle. As we cleared the station, I could still see police running around.

There were more Gendarmes at the next five or six stations and then, none. At the beginning of all this, we had removed our hats so that we would not stand out in the crowd. It was a bit like watching a movie; everything was happening so very quickly.

By the time we reached the terminus, there weren't many people left on the train. We loaded up and, with our map and two torches, found our way to the road which led to the camping ground.

* * *

The road was a long, tree-lined avenue, with the river on one side behind a high barbed-wire fence; and between the fence and the trees, was the footpath. We were looking into a black tunnel and there appeared to be no lighting. We changed our hats for our motorbike helmets, mainly to take some weight out of our rucksacks, as well as giving us some possible protection in the dark laneway. We set off with our eyes adjusted to the dark. We flicked our torches on alternately, to save batteries.

We moved at a brisk pace and from time to time, saw figures in the shadows but we kept moving. Eventually the lights of the campground came into view and it was only then, that we realised how big this place was.

It was now after midnight, when we went through the main gate to the reception desk where the English instructions read, 'Press the bell'. A man popped out from behind a table and stared at us.

We asked, "Can we camp here?"

He was very wary. Holding out his hand, he said, "Passports?"

We handed them to him. He studied them; then looked at us. Of course we looked nothing like the photos, with beards and all grubby.

Then he said, "Have you any money?"

We showed him our French francs (thanks to our bank manager), as well as our travellers cheques. He examined them, still not quite sure. He seemed to relax a little then and handed us some forms to fill in. We filled in the forms and paid for four nights.

Then he asked, "By which way, did you come to get here?"

We told him, "We walked along the tree lined avenue, from the railway station."

He rolled his eyes and said, "Nobody walks along there after dark, let alone at midnight. It is the mugging capital of Paris, if not France. You are lucky to be alive. It's a very bad place."

Keith and I looked at each other and said, "How horrible we look, all bearded and grubby. We are both so ugly at the moment, no one would possibly be interested."

But no one would have seen that, in the dark of the tunnel. We had both been very lucky.

* * *

We collected our gear and followed him up a rise to the back of the ground near the back fence, which overlooked the Seine. We were also close to an ablution block. A young Danish couple camped nearby, had one good look at us, dropped their tent and shifted away from us.

We now believed we must have the plague! Keith went first to the showers, while I looked after the tent and wrote up my diary ... I had plenty to write about. Keith returned, looking so like a new pin, I wouldn't have known him.

As I was leaving for the showers, Keith said, "You will be in for a surprise when you get in there."

I wasn't too sure what that meant but I soon found out. I walked into the shower and wash basin area ... and mirrors – I did get a surprise. I did not know the fellow in the mirror: he was filthy. Thick hair standing up on end, I was covered in grease and grime over the well-tanned, outdoors skin. All the creases on my face were filled with sweat and dirt, making me look as though I had black lines drawn across my face. The Genghis Khan beard didn't help either. The shirt and green trousers were bleached yellow in patches, making me appear to be in perfect camouflage gear. Now I understood why we were being avoided. It was then, I realised I didn't smell at all sweet either.

It was right into the shower ... and the run of water changed colour. That shower was the best I have ever had. I actually felt clean. I could now re-enter the tent with that other clean person.

The next day was fine and we washed our dust-caked clothes,

along with other things. With that done, we went via bus and Metro to explore the big city for six days, using our guide books.

* * *

I felt somewhat glad then, that Mirrabooka had broken down; since, looking at that mad traffic, I think we would have been run over ... and if that had happened, I would not now be writing this. With our own transport gone, we felt strangely alone. 'Mirra' had been one third of the team and now, she was turning into just a memory; with memories of other breakdowns – only then, they had been happening in front of some garage or an engineering workshop, along with tools to effect repairs.

The bulk of our travel had taken place well-away from main roads and the tourist beat, with little or no help available. Many were the times we had come out of rough country into a town, before 'Mirra' decided it was time for repairs.

Fuji had been on and off with us and I couldn't blame them; they probably regarded us as two wayward scooter nomads ... but they could not have possibly known of the adventures we had.

We'd had our spills on the scooter but with the exception of Keith's arm fracture, nothing else major happened ... and riding on roads paved with boulders, sand, gravel, ice, snow, mud, and diesel oil, somehow we survived. For myself, our brake pads had done a great job. Some of the mountain roads had been very steep and dangerous, as the locals would always remind us.

Keith, on numerous occasions after a long down-hill run, would say to me, "You took that a bit quick, didn't you?" What he didn't see, was my concentration on reading the road and where the front wheel was going. Soft sand usually put us over the handlebars. We wanted to see the world at ground level and we couldn't get much closer to the ground than on a scooter and still move. I've lost count of the number of tyres we went through; most of them weren't what you would call heavy-duty.

* * *

We had just returned to the camping ground after sightseeing. On entering reception, we ran into Ricardo from Barcelona, whom we had last seen in Ceylon and Madras. He had been on our leopard-spotting evening in Wilpattu National Park in Ceylon. Ricardo was now on his way home to Spain, after having spent some time teaching in India.

We decided to freshen up and go to dinner somewhere. We were told there was a nice place that served light curry close-by, overlooking the Seine. It sounded like a nice venue. I turned around and was surprised to see Derek, a South African from

Durban. The last time we had seen him, was in Lahore. Greetings were exchanged all round – this now made a party of four.

We found the restaurant and ate something we had all said, we would not touch again for a long time: a curry ... but it was mild, not like the ones we had once eaten. The only one missing from the gathering was Mirrabooka, who was sitting quietly at the railway station, waiting to board the train, then the ship, for the long voyage home.

Keith and I agreed that the whole trip had been quite an adventure: a real adventure. We filled our glasses and drank a toast to all of our past adventures ... and to the ones we were still to know nothing about.

Our camp in Paris ... sans Mirrabooka

Paris and the Eiffel Tower, Paris, France

Tourist boat on the Seine, Paris, France

Champs Elysees and the Arc de Triomphe, Paris, France

Keith browsing in the Left Bank, Paris, France

EPILOGUE ... POST-'MIRRA':

THE UK

After our long overland journey and the celebration of meeting up with friends on arriving in Paris, our thoughts changed to, "What's next".

Having seen as much of Paris as time and money allowed, we boarded the train for the ferry ride across the English Channel, arriving in London early the following morning.

The station master at Verdun had booked our scooter and us through to London, where we hoped we could get a passage back to Australia by ship. On enquiring about shipping to Australia, we found there was a three-month delay on bookings before a berth would become available. There were a lot of people on the move.

Keith had been to the UK before and was more interested now in getting a job, to earn some money.

Before leaving on our trip, I had put some money in the bank in London, in case I needed it at the end of the journey. Having not been here before, I thought I should put the money to good use and embark on an exploration of Britain. The scooter had storage in London, for we intended to take her home with us.

I had a youth hostel membership which would help me with my accommodation; so I set off for Scotland with the plan to work my way south, from John O'Groats to Land's End, using whatever transport might be available.

* * *

It started with an over-night bus trip to Edinburgh, through the industrial mid-lands; then the rolling green hills, dotted with farm houses and with black and white sheep, arriving next day in Edinburgh and missing the Military Tattoo by twelve hours. I had been looking forward to seeing the Tattoo but the delay with the buses had made that impossible. I did get to see the clean-up after the event and have a tour of the castle – which was most impressive.

I spent a lot of time looking around the city while using the big youth hostel at Bruntsfield. Then the rain, which had dogged us in Norway, had been looking for me ... and found me, from across the North Sea; just to let me know who was in charge. I tried to out-run it with the help of a navy man who got me as far as Perth.

After that, a kind truck driver in a Commer truck took me to Aviemore, where heather was in full bloom, brightening the landscape of lakes and streams, all held in place under a blanket of grey cloud. Although cloudy next day, it was a good day for walking the heather-lined road and little wee lochs. An Austin truck picked me up and took me to Inverness, where I had a tour of the castle on the Ness River. It was a good refuelling stop, with a good Irish stew for lunch. Walking out of town, I continued to be more impressed with the heather: it just got bigger and the colour more brilliant.

At the hostel at the foot of Ben Nevis, I met a party of climbers who were going to have a go at the mountain and I was invited to join the party. When we got to the base of the mountain, the cloud swirled in and Ben Nevis disappeared. Then the wind got up – it was no time to go climbing. With Ben Nevis out of the question, it was time to move on to Glencoe, which proved to be full of picture-postcard scenery. I stayed there four days, as there was lots to see and do.

The lady in charge of this hostel was a Mrs Fenny. She only needed a Viking helmet and a battle-axe; for she had the big-mama build to carry them. She ran the hostel like a tight ship and if anyone played up, they got to 'black-lead' the big wood stove. That stove was the best-looking stove in Scotland.

'Black lead' was a paste made up of Plumbago, graphite and soft, grey-black solids, used for stopping rust in cast-iron stoves.

The method of applying was, as we used to say, with plenty of 'elbow-grease'; i.e. rubbing hard, to get it into the metal. The down-side was that it was very difficult to get off the skin.

* * *

'Big Mamma' had organised two climbers from England to take a small party to look at the mountains, through a gorge with 610 metre-high cliffs. Past the Three Sisters, the wind in the gorge was so terrific we could barely stand upright. It was really wild country. Just then, the sun came out briefly as we passed rapids and waterfalls to a cave, where we had lunch. We walked to the head of the gorge, where it was at its best and so very spectacular.

Then the wind and rain started again. Trees were being blown- over sideways. We were now out of the gorge and moving down into open country, when we heard a loud noise and were startled to see a whole paling fence being blown down the hill towards us. We all scrambled for cover. I found a small boulder to cower behind but I had to keep my head down. I took a quick look at the others, who had all managed to find a large rock. Palings were flying past us, some smacking the rocks and shattering. It was like a wartime engagement.

When the fence had passed us, we stood up and looked around at the damage. Most of the trees were horizontal. Looking down into the valley, we saw a car towing a caravan driving along the road. The savage wind hit them, tearing the caravan from the car and rolling it along the road, smashing it to pieces. The wind had now stopped, as had the car. The driver got out and walked around the tangled mess, to find that everything was broken except for one window. He then proceeded to kick it in, to make the destruction total.

Back at the hostel, the evening meal was followed by a two-hour sing-song around the piano; then Scottish dancing accompanied by piano accordions and bagpipes, played by a group of Canadians who had brought their pipes with them. It was an hilarious evening. At 11.30 pm a gong sounded and everyone had to be in bed immediately – or it would be 'black-lead' the stove in the morning!

The rain and wind were still roaring the next day and everybody stayed inside. The roads were all blocked by fallen trees and cars were stranded ... but at the hostel all this was handled by another sing-song, followed by wild dancing until mid-night. They even had a Campbells versus McDonalds dance, in time with the shaking of the building.

***

The following day, with the cloud down, I walked out through the fallen trees and stranded cars, past roaring waterfalls and river gorges: all spectacular – then on, out into moor country, where the scenery was still dramatic. After Glencoe, the hostel that night was so quiet you could hear people change their minds!

At Loch Lomond, we had an old manor house for a hostel. The contrast in the accommodation made the travelling interesting. All the hostels I visited in the area were big on Highland dancing, each dance similar but also different. To get to the Trossachs, I had to go through Rob Roy country: very pretty but not as rugged as Glencoe. I would have liked to go climbing in these areas but it was still too wet and dangerous.

In Glasgow it was still raining and so for a change, I took in some shows. One had a cast of 75 dancers, full of colour and action. Getting out of Glasgow, I got lost and finished up at Ayr but I was happy with this, as I got to see the sheep-dog trials. I was rather conspicuous, wearing my 'Aussie' digger's hat and so was noticed by a reporter from a 'Visitors to Britain' newspaper. I was interviewed about my travels ... and they even paid me for the article!

I saw Robert Burns' cottage on the road to Stanraer, where sheep were grazing right to the shoreline. This was where the ferry left for Ireland and, on arriving at the jetty, a trip to Ireland didn't look so good ... there was a black sky and a high wind bringing breakers into the inlet. The ferry was bobbing around like a cork and would-be passengers were waiting to hear if the ferry was going to go or not. After an hour, an announcement was made – because of the weather conditions, there would be no ferry departures for 48 hours ... such a pity, as we could see Ireland out under the black sky and looking quite close. I moved into the local hostel for the night, along with a lot of other people and the topic was ... the weather!

* * *

With Ireland out of the question, I set out on foot in the rain and fog the next day. I had covered a fair distance, when I was asked "Do you want a lift in a pie delivery van? I am heading for Derwent Water."

"Yes, please." I helped him deliver his pies and while at it, I also had a good lunch.

I said farewell to Scotland and, on re-entering England, got a lift with a chap who was off to climb Great Gable, 899 metres high. The track led up to Sty Head Pass, the head of the

Derwent River; and up over cliff faces covered with climbers. Lunch was under some organ pipes with spectacular views and then, on up scree slopes, to Kern Knotts, Napes Needle and Scarfell Pike, at 978 metres. We crossed ridges and stone walls to an old graphite mine, dating back to the 1700's, where we went down a way and found stools, tools and footprints of the early miners. It was very wet down there.

Calling it a day, I received a lift on a motorbike to Keswick. It was one of the best outings I had had for some while, because of the weather and because it was good to stretch the legs.

* * *

At Stratford, I booked for an evening performance at the William Shakespeare Memorial Theatre, for just two shillings and sixpence. First, I had to go to the hostel and clean up ... that still meant, in what I was wearing ... except they were now, clean. Romeo and Juliet was the play and I joined up with a South African chap. Our booking was for standing-room only, which meant that we had to stand for the whole performance ... and that finished at 11 pm. We enjoyed every minute of it, which said a lot about the quality of the performance.

Leaving the theatre, we had coffee and a snack. Ian went off to his lodgings and myself, off to the hostel, which I now found to be locked up for the night, it being so late. I walked to the park and found a long seat for a bed. I had only just got myself settled, when it started to rain. The only cover I could see, was under a jetty on the river. At the jetty, there were rowing boats moored; so I climbed into one of these and paddled under the jetty out of the rain. I settled into the boat and fell asleep, only to be woken up before dawn by four swans who poked their heads into the boat and gave me a very loud honking, which all but lifted me out of the boat. I was now wide awake but stayed in the boat until the rain stopped.

* * *

Back in London and in Keith's flat, I made the most of it and visited tourist spots from the Palace to museums, where I spent a lot of time. I caught up with the scooter and gave it an overdue clean up ... it was really filthy, after travelling all those miles.

It was there that I met an archaeologist, who was doing some work on Roman diggings and he invited me to join him, which proved to be yet another highlight. We got down as far as Stonehenge, where he showed me Cerne Grant: a huge carving in limestone, made by ancient Britains, 4000 years ago. We looked at a Roman aqueduct eight miles long, a Roman amphitheatre and buildings, plus thirty earth mounds and forts built by Celts, the ancient Britains. I was also shown where convicts bound for Australia were held awaiting transportation.

On my way to Torquay on the south coast, I found myself travelling with a chap who fixed TV sets. We arrived quite late when he dropped me near my hostel. To get to it, I had a long walk up an easement clothed in trees and turning the walkway into another dark tunnel, I had to use my torch to find the road. I was about halfway along, when large dogs attacked the other side of the fence, making me leap in the air and I half-expected to be eaten. When I finally came to the hostel, a beautiful manor house, I was warmly greeted and I told them of my encounter with the dogs.

They laughed and said, "You found Agatha Christie's place. She is seldom there but she has good security."

* * *

Before making my way to Torquay, I had been walking toward Dartmoor. It was late afternoon and with the bad weather, it was fast getting dark. A Land Rover pulled up beside me. The army officers inside asked me where I was going.

I said, "To the hostel," whereupon they offered me a lift. They were concerned about my walking alone in moor country, in bad weather and the chance of getting lost in the fog.

They asked, "Do you have a torch?" ... I showed them mine.

They said, "We will take that and give you a better one. Also, here is a survival kit. We hope you don't have to use it."

With my new torch and survival kit, I was delivered at the hostel and thanked them for looking after me. It turned out that they were in fact, SAS.

At Dartmouth, I saw a monument to the 'Mayflower's departure for America and at Plymouth, a monument to Francis Drake, along with some forts: all quite informative. On the way to Mevagissey, a pretty, hilly Cornish fishing village, I stopped to look at the china clay-works. Now walking, I had plenty of time to look and take things in, as the countryside was picturesque with farm houses. Walking through the village, I was stopped by a Mr Alan, who invited me to have morning tea with him and his wife; they were both so very friendly.

* * *

The hilly countryside, with narrow roads and alley ways, made for interesting walking. I never knew what was going to be around the next bend; but one bend had a hotel which served fish and chips – and they loaded me up well for the next day.

I obtained a lift on a coke truck, driven by a dour Cornish man who believed in 'the little people'. He showed me where they live and advised the best time to come and see them. I kept looking around the truck to see if I could see one. He was very convincing and I did my best to keep a straight face. He actually stopped on a little bridge and pointed to a rock-strewn hill, which he believed had caves to house some of them. We eventually got to his destination at St Michel's Mount.

Sixty-odd years later, I can still see him sitting behind the steering wheel, all covered in a layer of black coke dust, talking to me. Maybe the little people were truly real – or had he just been having me on?

I went past a number of old manor houses surrounded by high stone walls, looking like something from another era. I walked into Penzance, where I was told pirates used to live – but only if you believed in Gilbert and Sullivan! I found in Penzance that they made the biggest and most-delicious Cornish pasties.

Late afternoon, I walked on to Land's End and watched the sun set over the Atlantic Ocean. I bought fish and chips for dinner and there, was joined by the driver of a Jag. He asked me where I was going and then offered to drop me off at the youth hostel. I arrived in a brand-new, red Jaguar. The wind was howling and the rain had started. I arrived, wind-blown but dry.

* * *

Next morning, I went exploring and found the area was full of old tin mines which would have been worked many centuries ago. Cornwall had been famous for its tin mines and for the miners who worked them. These men were recruited world-wide for their skills.

That morning, the rain was really savage as I was walking to St Ives but a baker kindly offered me a lift. The seas were huge and had to be seen to be believed, with lots of land disappearing in the spray. I felt I should quickly get out of St Ives before it disappeared into the boiling seas.

Walking around the back streets, I was met by a Methodist pastor, who enquired where I was going.

I said, "In the general direction of Bristol," ... not really knowing where I was going.

He asked, "How would Bodmin suit?"

I said, "That would be good."

It was adjacent to Bodmin Moor and I knew that there was a hostel, where I could take refuge from the wind and rain.

* * *

On my way to Tintagel, I was given a lift by a chap who owned a pub and thought his dad might like to meet me, as he had been to Australia. When I found the hostel there, it was located on the cliff-line and was closed due to the weather. I noticed the cycle shed, which was away from the main building and was open. At that point the heavens opened up and it poured. I jumped into the cycle shed and decided that this was home for the night. I had my good torch and made a bed which turned out to be quite comfortable ... and I was dry and out of the rain. The one thing I had to do in a hurry, was barricade the door against the wind. Now remembering that building, the structure had appeared quite strong – I hoped it was 'super-strong'. In spite of all this, I slept very-well. As I had my breakfast of fruit and bread, the wind was still belting the building.

I walked eight or ten kilometres from the town, to be picked up by a couple of Londoners. They were on holiday in Cornwall and invited me to join them exploring the area. I thought it was very kind of them and happily accepted.

Just south of Bude, on a back road, we got caught up in a fox hunt. We had the lot – horses, hounds and huntsmen, including a bugler, who altogether stopped any traffic on this narrow, hedge-lined, unsealed road. How we got onto this road hadn't been in the plan but a wrong turn can quickly change everything. Now we were part of a fox hunt ... in a car.

We were on the uphill side of the road and had a good viewing position, watching the hounds on the scent, horses and riders cantering across the road in hot pursuit. From our viewing position, it was all terribly dramatic and complete with sound effects – better than TV!

The Londoners thanked me for coming with them and said, "If we hadn't given you a lift, we would have missed this."

From the hunt, we went to Clovelly, a small fishing village in Devon, only accessible by mules ... a wonderful, quaint little place. From there, it was on to Westward Ho and Appledore – both seaside resorts. The beaches were mostly shingles. Then came Bideford, another big port town; afterwards, we drove on to Barnstaple, where they dropped me off on the other side of town.

I alighted from their car only to be offered another lift, by the driver of a fruit truck which was going to Linton. We were now in rough country again: hilly wild gorges, high cliff- lines, fronting the ocean and monstrous seas. Ten years prior to our visit, the area had suffered big floods and many people had drowned.

I walked up a long hill to a small village outside the town and was offered a lift to Minehead, in Somerset and from there, crossed the moor into 'Doon' country – a very pretty coastline with lovely rolling hills. Since the hostel there was closed, I managed to find myself a very nice B and B.

I bypassed the big city of Bristol and travelled on to Bath, where I went walk-about and looked at the Roman history of the city.

There followed another quick trip back to Stonehenge, after which it was off to Wales, to meet the Jenkins family at Cymmer, just north of Port Talbot, adjoining the Rhondda Valley. I had previously met them at Stratford.

* * *

Del and Ayless with family, had migrated to Queensland (to Kilcoy to be exact) but they couldn't handle the climate and so, went back to Wales. Del was a carpenter and the undertaker for the district and I found his workshop most interesting. Aside from the usual things to be found in a workshop, one side of his was stacked with coffins – empty ones – all of different sizes and shapes.

Something much amused me the weekend after I arrived, when he took me to a rugby match. Before we arrived there, we first had to collect a load of coffins. It was a good match and very entertaining, for when the players got into the flow, the singing started. Five hundred Welsh men were now singing their heads off in full harmony.

A short, barrel-chested Welsh man beside me said, "You are not singing."

I replied, "I am busy listening."

He then replied, "Sing! It doesn't matter ... no one else is listening."

The match finished and we didn't have to use any of the coffins ... but they did have to be delivered on to another village.

* * *

The next day, I was taken to see yet another fox hunt but this time I got to see the whole event, from saddling of the horses to the actual hunt. I met two other stray people like myself and we decided to blend into the landscape.

While watching the horses and hounds getting ready for the event, the call to arms was sounded: the hounds went first, followed by the cavalry. One of our party owned what could be described as a mini-moke, which we all piled into. The driver was from the district and knew the highways and byways. I think he had definitely done this before, as he drove on tracks not visible to the eye to a vantage point where we could see all the action. We watched them thread their way across the countryside and we could hear the distant hounds.

After what seemed like a long time, a red ball of fur burst through the hedge, right in front of the moke. He seemed to be considering sheltering under the car but he changed his mind and took off down the hill. The huntsmen arrived and the lead man pointed enquiringly down the hill to us but our driver pointed the other way.

It was time to leave, since it was becoming a bit crowded. The moke took off along another track and soon it was all behind us. We drove on back to the parking lot and waited there in a tea room, enjoying an afternoon tea. Then my transport arrived and we all went our various ways. It had all been very interesting ... and I did hope that the fox had got away. Some time later, I did hear that they had never caught it.

I spent the next day helping Del with some odd-jobs. During this time, he also took me along to their local choir practice which proved hugely-entertaining, with such a blending of male voices as one could only ever expect to encounter in Wales.

* * *

I now had a firm departure time for the ship: in two weeks. I then made a few quick trips around the country to say my goodbyes – to Newcastle, Sheffield, Wales, Chester, Plymouth and London.

When we loaded the scooter, we were surprised to see the 'Queen Mary' moored behind us. The ship looked massive.

The weather which had followed us across the North Sea, England, Wales and Scotland, was still with us. Our departure was put back twice before we were allowed to sail but only after the 'Queen Mary' went first. We watched, as ten tugs pulled her out into the channel and then she disappeared into the mist.

We were finally on our way home.

* * *

On our arrival in Melbourne, we were approached by a man wanting to buy our scooter. He was a collector and had been trying to get hold of our model for his collection. We told him we would think about it, because it was booked through to Brisbane and could not be off-loaded in Melbourne.

Keith and I discussed the offer. We had intended to take it home and recondition it ourselves but back home, the picture had changed – we both had to start work. We asked ourselves, when would we get time to work on the scooter? The answer became clear: we should take the offer.

Keith immediately went back to work, while I decided to do something different and finished up working for a timber company. I then got married and the scooter became only a memory. It had served us well but reality can be very blunt ... and it was time to let it go. Going to a new owner who was a collector, it would have a dignified retirement.

Finally, the Norwegian weather men in Oslo were spot on with their forecast: that northern Europe would have the wettest summer season in 100 years. The rain, snow and ice had followed us from northern Europe to the UK and in doing so, had given us an adventure with a difference, coping with all that rain, snow and ice. We had met a lot of very interesting people, some of whom went out of their way to help us with repairs to the scooter and finally, we had made lots of friends along the way.

Keith and I had travelled the full distance and I can't remember one cross word passing between us. We would simply work our way through a problem. We were both, very easy going.

When Keith had broken his arm in Ceylon, I'd asked him how he felt about carrying on with his arm in plaster, from the shoulder to the wrist.

He'd said, "I am not going to miss this trip, for quids."

The whole journey had been one big adventure, from beginning to end.

AND THIS WAS ... THE END

On board the 'Bretagne' ... Returning Home

Big Ben & the Houses of Parliament, Westminster, London

Edinburgh Castle, Edinburgh, Scotland

A Vale in Glencoe, Scotland

Loch Lomond in southern Scotland

Robert Burn's Cottage in Alloway, on the road to Stranraer, Scotland

From Grate Gable, looking west to Wastwater ... the Lake District, Cumbria, England

Sarsen stones at Stonehenge, Wiltshire, southwest England

The Pirate Inn at Penzance, Cornwall, England

Pig track on rim of Snowdon, northwest Wales

As we head for home... the Queen Mary at berth, Southampton, England

ADDENDUM
A PHOTOGRAPHIC SUMMARY:
FROM ISTANBUL TO SOUTHAMPTON

The crossing to Corinth, 'Mirabooka' on the deck, Greece

Looking towards Meteora, central Greece

A valley in Yugoslavia near the Dinaric Alps

The Dinaric Alps in Yugoslavia, along the coast of the Adriatic Sea

Kotor in Montenegro ... near Dubrovnik, Yugoslavia

The Schonbrunn Palace in Vienna, Austria

Kaiser Franz Joseph Glacier, near Heiligenblut, Austria

The Alps near the Brenner Pass, Austria

Interlaken in the Canton of Bern, Bernese Oberland, Switzerland

Bernese Oberland, west-central Switzerland

High in the Swiss Alps

'Mirrabooka' in the Alps, Southern Germany

The Rhine Falls & hydro-generation, near Zurich on the Swiss-German border

Brandenburg Gate, West Berlin, Germany

Russian War Memorial, East Berlin, East Germany

Copenhagen, Denmark

A church in southern Norway

Thor Heyerdahl's 'Kon Tiki' raft in its museum in Oslo, Norway

Stockholm from the 'Vandrarahem' deck, Sweden

A road bridge in Sweden

A canal barge in Amsterdam, Holland

Houses on the Amstel River, Amsterdam, Holland

A windmill at Kinderdijk, near Rotterdam, South Holland

Downtown in Brussels, Belgium

Cottage with a thatched roof outside Brussels, Belgium

The Arc de Triomphe overlooking Champs Elysees, Paris, France

The Eiffel Tower overlooking Paris, France

Paris seen from the Eiffel Tower, Paris, France

Tower Bridge from the Embankment, London, England

St James' Palace, The Mall, central London, England

Firth of Forth Bridge, east of Edinburgh, Scotland

Inverness in the Scottish Highlands, Central Scotland

Derwent Waters Valley, The Lake District, mid-west England

Climbing Napes Needle on Grate Gable, Cumbria in the Lakes District, England

Entry to the Mersey Tunnel, Liverpool, mid-west England

Chester in mid-west England, near the northern Welsh Border

Chester Cathedral, in the city of Chester, Cheshire, England

Caernarfon Castle, Gwynedd, north - west Wales

Climbers' camps in the Snowdon Valley, Gwynedd in north-west Wales

From the foot of Snowdon, looking down the valley

At the fox-hunt in Wales

Cheddar Gorge in the Mendip Hills, Somerset, England

Petticoat Lane markets, Spitalfields in London's East End, England

wn

24, 1961

Blocs: Little London, Chichester
(Phone: Chichester 3333)

FOR ALL
**MUSICAL
INSTRUMENTS**
Consult the
MUSICAL EXPERTS
STORRYS
of CHICHESTER
83, NORTH STREET

THREE PENCE

From Australia To Chichester On A Motor Scooter

Australian Mr. Edsel Ward.
—O.S. 9345

WITH a deep sun tan and weatherbeaten look as the most obvious souvenirs, a 30-year-old Australian adventurer is at present "recuperating" in Chichester after a scooter ride.

But this was no ordinary ride. It took him through 24 countries on a 21,000-mile journey from his home in Brisbane.

"It has been a wonderful experience," Mr. Edsel Ward said, as he relaxed at the Saltmill Road, Fishbourne, home of the Rickard family, where he is staying for a few days before returning to Australia by liner.

"I had many strange and wonderful experiences on the journey, but the lesson that was really brought home to me is that people are the same the world over."

Friendliness

He said: "Regardless of race, creed, or colour, I met the same friendliness and help everywhere."

Mr. Ward's two-wheeled ride to adventure began in December last year, when he left his native Australia with fellow Brisbanian Mr. Keith Bassett (34).

After a sea voyage to Colombo, the intrepid adventurers toured Ceylon and then made their way by ferry to southern India.

During an extensive tour of the Indian sub-continent they visited Calcutta and Madras, Darjeeling, Delhi, and Lahore. They also spent a considerable period in the Himalaya foothills of East Nepal, and visited Katmandu.

"The Himalayas are a breath-taking sight," Mr. Ward declared. "At times the views defied description."

Trouble Spot

After a spot of trouble with Afghanistan border guards, the travellers headed into the vast desert wastes of Persia.

"We tried to enter Afghanistan, but the frontier guards did not seem at all keen on the idea," said Mr. Ward. Following a memorable stay in Teheran, they made their way across the desert to Turkey, and from Istanbul into Greece and Yugoslavia.

"The people of Yugoslavia were among the friendliest I met on our journey, but they had a horror of people in uniform," said Mr. Ward. He had personal experience of this when "booked" for a parking offence by a grim-looking Yugoslav policeman.

"It is the first time I have ever been pinched for parking by a policeman carrying an automatic rifle," he chuckled. "I got the impression it was a case of pay up — or else."

Break Down

The couple's European travels took them through countries as far apart as Finland and Italy, East Germany and Belgium, before their scooter eventually broke down outside Paris.

On arrival in England, the friends split up temporarily and, minus his scooter — which was stored in a London garage — Mr. Ward hitchhiked his way around Britain, making friends in Scotland and Wales in the process.

At the week-end he arrived in Chichester and announced: "I like this city very much. It has a quiet beauty about it."

At the end of the month he will rejoin Mr. Bassett in London and they will travel home by luxury liner.

Speaking of his experiences on the journey Mr. Ward said: "My narrowest escape occurred in Persia. I was collecting firewood when I came face to face with a gigantic mamba snake. It coiled itself to spring at me but slithered away as I made a desperate grab for my machete."

Trip Cost £650

Estimating that the entire trip had cost him £650, Mr. Ward explained that he would return to his old job as a plasterer when he eventually reached Brisbane again.

Of Britain he had this to say: "The people over here are extremely well mannered and a lot more friendly than some people think at home. I have not seen much of the traditional British reserve."

Driver Denied Accident Was His Fault

AN Emsworth company director, who was alleged to have driven into the side of a car in Chichester, was fined £5 by Chichester Magistrates on Wednesday.

The defendant, Mr. Albert Joseph Lewis, of Lucerne, Horndean Road, Emsworth, pleaded not guilty to driving without due care and attention.

Announcing the fine, the presiding Chairman, Mr. Stanley Roth said to defendant: "The onus was on you as you were coming from a car park on to a highway."

Mr. Frederick Norris Uden, of Uden's Stockbridge Road Chichester, said that he was driving from East Pallant into New Town when he saw the defendant stationary in the entrance to the Central Car Park.

"He was stationary when I saw him, but as I passed the car park he appeared to drive into me."

Defendant said he was driving his car out of the car park. There were cars waiting for him to clear the entrance, so he proceeded slowly to turn right when a car past and scraped him from behind.

"The first I knew about it was when my father said 'Look out, he is going to hit you,'" said Mr. Lewis.

Clipping from a Chichester newspaper 1961, Chichester, West Sussex, England

www.ingramcontent.com/pod-product-compliance
Lightning Source LLC
Chambersburg PA
CBHW071714090426
42738CB00009B/1771